YORKSHIRE ENGINE COMPANY

Sheffield's Locomotive Manufacturer

Tony Vernon

YORKSHIRE ENGINE COMPANY

SHEFFIELD'S LOCOMOTIVE MANUFACTURER

TONY VERNON

By the same author:

Archibald Sturrock: Pioneer Locomoive Engineer, The History Press, 2006.

First published 2008

The History Press
The Mill, Brimscombe Port
Stroud, Gloucestershire, GL5 2QG
www.thehistorypress.co.uk

Reprinted 2008, 2009, 2014

© Tony Vernon, 2008

The right of Tony Vernon to be identified as the Author
of this work has been asserted in accordance with the
Copyrights, Designs and Patents Act 1988.

All rights reserved. No part of this book may be reprinted
or reproduced or utilised in any form or by any electronic,
mechanical or other means, now known or hereafter invented,
including photocopying and recording, or in any information
storage or retrieval system, without the permission in writing
from the Publishers.
British Library Cataloguing in Publication Data.
A catalogue record for this book is available from the British Library.

ISBN 978 0 7524 4530 4

Typesetting and origination by The History Press
Printed in Great Britain

Contents

Introduction		6
Chapter 1	Establishing the Company, 1865–1871	8
Chapter 2	Experiments and Failure, 1872–1883	22
Chapter 3	The Hampson Years, 1884–1906	36
Chapter 4	New Management and New Ventures, 1906–1919	50
Chapter 5	The Interwar Years, 1919–1939	64
Chapter 6	Second World War and the End of Steam, 1939–1956	79
Chapter 7	The Final Years, 1956–1965	103
Appendices		
A	Plan of Works	135
B	Yorkshire Engine Order Book – Steam, Electric and Tramway Locomotives	135
C	Yorkshire Engine Order Book – Diesel Locomotives	143
Bibliography		156
Index		158

Introduction

The Yorkshire Engine Company was Sheffield's only locomotive manufacturer. Although one of the smaller firms in the industry, it produced a number of novel steam and diesel designs. Its willingness to experiment with new ventures, including the manufacture of cars, sometimes threatened its existence. Locomotive overhauls, the building of boilers and the supply of mining machinery were all part of its product range for many years.

The Yorkshire Engine Co. survived for a hundred years until 1965, largely because its management was innovative and willing to offer a range of engineering services to local firms whenever locomotive business was unavailable or unprofitable. It built a total of almost 1,200 steam and diesel locomotives, about eighty of which survive mainly on preserved railways and in museums in 2008. More than fifty years after closure, around twenty Yorkshire Engine diesels continue in regular operational use in steelworks in Lincolnshire and South Yorkshire, a tribute to the quality of products the company made.

My own interest in the firm developed as a result of research for my biography of Archibald Sturrock, the Great Northern Locomotive Engineer, who opened the East Coast main line and is often remembered for his auxiliary steam tenders. Sturrock was my great-great grandfather and was closely involved with the founding of the Yorkshire Engine Co. I had a further reason to be curious about the history of the firm; I worked for the United Steel Companies in the early 1960s, when the Yorkshire Engine Co. was part of the group.

This book would not have been possible without the records and photographs held in the Sheffield Archives. I would like to thank the staff of the Sheffield Archives for their considerable help over more than five years. I am also most grateful for the assistance provided by the late Reg Carter, librarian of the Stephenson Locomotive Society, Ivor Thomas, librarian, and Ian Bendall, archivist of the Industrial Railway Society. The handbooks of the Industrial Railway Society were invaluable sources of information. The archivists of the Institution of Mechanical Engineers and the Institution of Civil Engineers also assisted with information on former members involved with the Yorkshire Engine Co.

The story of the final years of the Yorkshire Engine Co. would have been difficult to write without help from those who worked at the Yorkshire Engine Co. and their families. As a result of a letter published in the *Rotherham Advertiser*, I received over a dozen letters and many photographs and was able to meet a number of former employee and others with a great knowledge of the business. I should like to record my thanks to Roy Bassendale, Vera Brown, John Christmas, Dennis Harding, Sir Simon Benton Jones, Bernard Ledger, David Love, Mick Norman, Hedley Oldfield, Peter Briddon, Jim Ramsden, Duncan Reed, Jean Rose and Harry Stenton. Particular thanks are due to Andrew Briddon and Andrew Hurrell for help with the diesel locomotives and to Derek Penney and Peter Hawkins for much information about the later years at the Yorkshire Engine Co. All four supplied many documents and photographs and were good enough to read the last two chapters of the book and make valuable corrections and suggestions. I also want to thank Howard Turner, who introduced me to Derek and Peter, and kindly read the whole manuscript. Responsibility for any remaining errors is mine.

Thanks are also due to Corus Engineering Steels and their Head of Transport, Mick Morris, for arranging a visit to see Yorkshire Engine Co. locomotives at work at Aldwarke and to Chesterfield Special Cylinders and their Managing Director, John Hayward, for giving up time to show me around the former Yorkshire Engine Co. works at Meadowhall.

The illustrations are a key part of the book. I am most grateful to those who gave permission for their own photographs and those from their collections to be reproduced. The source of each illustration is noted alongside the caption. A number of photographs were taken from an undated *Locomotive Magazine* supplement on the Yorkshire Engine Co. and are marked LM. Others have been taken from two Yorkshire Engine catalogues.

I hope this book will encourage readers to take an interest in surviving Yorkshire Engine Co. locomotives. Sheffield residents can visit the Kelham Island Industrial Museum to see one of the first two Yorkshire Engine diesels or have a look at the photographs in the Sheffield archives (YEC 3–5). A visit to the Appleby Frodingham Railway Preservation Society in Scunthorpe provides an opportunity to see Yorkshire Engine Co. diesels at work in their original setting. The appendices list the location of many surviving Yorkshire Engine Co. steam and diesel locomotives in the UK and abroad. Checks should be made before arranging a visit, as locomotives are sometimes moved and several have recently been scrapped.

Tony Vernon
August 2008

Note to the 2014 reprint

Since the first publication of this book in 2008, the number of surviving Yorkshire Engine diesel locomotives has reduced from an estimated sixty-seven in 2008 to an estimated sixty-one in 2014. Of these, twenty-three are based on operational sites of Tata (formerly Corus) Steel in South Yorkshire, Lincolnshire, South Wales and North Yorkshire. Some of these Tata locomotives are out of use or being retained for spares. Other Yorkshire Engine locomotives can be found on preserved railways around Britain. A revised Appendix C provides updated information on the location of surviving Yorkshire Engine Diesel locomotives. The list includes one addition. The remains of YE2771 were identified at Matthews Ridge, Guyana some two years ago.

The number of surviving Yorkshire Engine steam locomotives is thought to have remained unchanged at thirteen. YE2521 has moved from Barrow Hil, Derbyshire to 'Rocks by Rail', Rutland.

I

Establishing the Company
1865–1871

Drivers leaving the M1 at junction 34 for the Meadowhall shopping complex must pass the buildings which once housed the Yorkshire Engine Co. Constructed in 1865, the much-refurbished buildings are now occupied by the long-established engineering firm Chesterfield Special Cylinders. The railway line over which the Yorkshire Engine Co. tested its locomotives is now a public path. The station to the north of the works at Blackburn is derelict but the former Wincobank & Meadowhall station, now just Meadowhall, is busy with shoppers travelling by train and 'super tram' to the adjacent shops.

Discussions about the development of a locomotive manufacturing plant in the Sheffield area were instigated by the Hon W.G. Eden in 1864. Eden was a retired diplomat, a director of the Manchester, Sheffield & Lincolnshire Railway (MSLR) and Chairman of the South Yorkshire Railway. He lived near Doncaster and was a friend of Archibald Sturrock, Locomotive Engineer of the Great Northern Railway (GNR). Eden appears to have been impressed by Sturrock's invention of the auxiliary or steam tender. This was a supplementary engine which drew steam from the main locomotive boiler to drive the wheels of the tender. Eden asked Sturrock to be the Chairman of the new company, when freed from his responsibilities with the GNR.

Sturrock was a wealthy man, having been left over £50,000 by his second wife. Although aged only forty-eight in 1864, he was able to contemplate retirement from the GNR and was willing to invest in the new venture. He wrote to his old friend, Daniel Gooch, Locomotive Superintendent and subsequently Chairman of the Great Western Railway (GWR):

> It would have given me pleasure to have been engaged with you in a limited company as not only would it have kept up old associations but that I have no doubt it would also have substantially benefited me. I can not now however for I am as deep in trading concerns as I think it prudent to be… I am pledged to embark in another manufacturing concern, similar to Tayleurs, on certain conditions, which are now under negotiation. Such renders it inappropriate for me to join any similar concern. I may mention to you that my late arrangement of auxiliary tenders has led to the said engagement on my part. I inform you of this to appraise you of the bona fides of my present interest.[1]

Gooch was involved with Charles Tayleur & Co., which became The Vulcan Foundry Ltd in 1864.

Other members of the group formed to set up Sheffield's first and only locomotive manufacturer included Thomas Rawson Barker, a lead merchant, who was on the South Yorkshire and MSLR boards with Eden, and Charles Sacré, the Engineer and Locomotive Superintendent of the MSLR. Charles Sacré had been a member of Sturrock's team on the GNR before securing his post on the MSLR. He was also involved with Sturrock in developing the auxiliary or steam tender. The Managing Director post was to be filled by Alfred Sacré, Charles's younger brother. Alfred held the post of Manager of the Peterborough locomotive department of the GNR, the post once filled by Charles. Alfred left the GNR and took up his new post in May 1865.

The promoters of the company considered £200,000 was needed to meet the costs of building and equipping the factory and for working capital. By 6 April 1865, when David Chadwick, a local accountant, wrote to potential shareholders asking for subscriptions, £120,000 had been promised. The minimum

Exterior of Meadowhall works probably shortly after construction. (Sheffield Archives)

The original brickwork of the Meadowhall works remains under the new cladding in February 2008. The railway line where locomotives were tested has become a long-distance path for cyclists and walkers. (Author)

Above left: *Archibald Sturrock in 1866. (Author's Collection)*

Above right: *Charles Sacré, the Engineer and Locomotive Superintendent of the Manchester Sheffield & Lincolnshire Railway, was Consulting Engineer for the construction of the Yorkshire Engine plant at Meadowhall. (Institution of Civil Engineers)*

subscription was fifty £100 shares or £5,000 to be paid up in tranches as the works was built. Sturrock and the two Sacré brothers each took £5,000 worth of shares. The letter advised investors that a Managing Director would be appointed who, with the approval of the board, would hire and fire and set wages. He would be able to enter into contracts conjointly with any two directors.

Eden took the chair at the preliminary meeting of the company at the Victoria Hotel, Sheffield on 22 April 1865. Sturrock was present plus both Sacrés. It was agreed that Charles Sacré should be appointed Consulting Engineer, for which he was to receive a fee of £300. Sturrock and George Wilson, another director, would also advise on the construction of the works. As Managing Director, Alfred was to receive £500 a year initially to be increased to £1,000, plus a bonus of 1 per cent of profits above 10 per cent. He was on a five-year contract. W.C. Stephens was to be appointed Secretary on £400 a year. The Works Manager was to be Robert Hampson; he was a twenty-eight-year-old former draughtsman who had worked with Sturrock monitoring the construction of GNR engines at Neilsons.

The extent to which the promoters had investigated the market is unclear. Hunslet had been established in Leeds the previous year on a site once used by E.B. Wilson of the Railway Foundry. Leeds had three other locomotive manufacturers at the time. Kitson had been established in 1835 as the Airedale Foundry, Manning Wardle had opened in 1858 and Hudswell Clarke in 1860. It may well have been thought that, if Leeds could support four locomotive manufacturers, Sheffield could justify at least one.

Alfred estimated the cost of building and equipping the works would be £126,427, if the plant was to be capable of producing two engines a week. By the time John Tomlinson, author of *Stories and Sketches relating to Yorkshire*, was taken round the works by Stephens and Hampson in 1866, he was told the plant was capable of producing 150 locomotives a year or three per week.[2] He was also led to believe the plant was costing £250,000 to build. The predictions for output proved to be optimistic.

By the second meeting of the board on 24 May 1865 £161,000 of shares had been taken up and it was agreed to seek subscriptions for the remaining shares from those who could be useful to the company. Sturrock was again present and suggested which items of machinery from Alfred Sacre's list should be purchased first. He visited manufacturers with Alfred to select machinery.

The May meeting expressed regret that Sturrock would not immediately take up the Chairmanship, but placed it at his disposal when he was ready to accept. In the meanwhile Eden remained Chairman and Sturrock continued to attend most board meetings and to work with Charles and Alfred Sacré on the design and construction of the factory. Sturrock formally joined the board in May 1866, five months after agreeing with the GNR that he would retire at the end of December 1866. He was elected Chairman of the Yorkshire Engine Co. on 10 January 1867. Forty-one shareholders had taken up all 2,000 shares.

By June 1865 tenders had been received for both buildings and machinery. Craven Brothers, a local Sheffield firm, secured the contract for the buildings. Machinery orders were spread amongst a number of suppliers, many of whom had taken shares in the business. The plant was built on a 22-acre site in open country at what was then known as Blackburn. The site is about two miles from Rotherham and three from the centre of Sheffield. It adjoined the South Yorkshire, MSLR and Midland lines. A horse and carriage were acquired to take the management from the office in Bank Street, Sheffield to the works. Forty-four-room and forty-five-room cottages were built for the workers.

Sturrock, Alfred Sacré and Barker formed a Stores Committee to oversee purchases. Hunt & Sacré were appointed London agents to develop contacts with customers. The agents would receive between 0.5 per cent and 2 per cent of the value of each order. Edward Sacré, joint managing partner of Hunt & Sacré and brother of Charles and Alfred, thus became involved. By 30 May 1867 the works was largely complete and machinery installed.[3]

Once Sturrock was installed as Chairman, Eden took on the Deputy role from Barker. Board days were busy. The Stores Committee met at 10.30, the Finance Committee at 12 noon and the board proper immediately after lunch. The Sheffield and Rotherham Bank managed the firm's accounts and agreed an overdraft facility of £30,000, subject to appropriate security.[4]

The market for locomotives was sound in 1865 and early 1866. The Yorkshire Engine Co. received enquiries from both home and overseas railways including the London, Chatham & Dover, the Seville and Malaga, the East Indian and the Great Indian Peninsula. The first order was placed by the GNR, whilst Sturrock was still in charge of the GNR's locomotive department.

The growth of the GNR's passenger traffic had lead to longer trains, which Sturrock's engines could handle only with difficulty. To maintain its reputation for good timekeeping, heavier trains must be divided in two. In the light of this Sturrock advised the GNR board he needed six more passenger engines.[5] The board agreed to obtain tenders for six 7ft singles from 'some of the best houses'. The Yorkshire Engine Co. was included on the list.

Tenders were opened on 9 January 1866. John Fowler of Leeds, now managed by Sturrock's former Works Manager Fred Parker, offered the best price of £2,890 and agreed to deliver three engines by 31 August 1866. The Yorkshire Engine Co.'s tender was the second most competitive of the ten at £2,950. Alfred Sacré was called in to the GNR board and agreed to drop his price to £2,890 and deliver one locomotive by October and two more in November 1866. At the same meeting, the Chairman Col. Packe announced that Sturrock was to retire in the next twelve to eighteen months and would be succeeded by Patrick Stirling.

A month later Sturrock had doubts about the suitability of six additional 7ft singles. He advised the GNR board that he wished to change to a four-wheeled coupled formation, 'if you decide to try the experiment'.[6] He estimated the extra cost to be £100 to £150. He expected the coupled engines to climb the banks more easily, but overall probably not be better than the singles originally proposed. The extra cost was agreed with both manufacturers at £175.

The change in specification from 2-2-2 to 2-4-0 can not have caused much trouble to the Yorkshire Engine Co., for the works was in no state to commence engine building. Foundations for the machinery were not laid till May 1866. The 2-4-0 express passenger engines, known as the 264 class, were Sturrock's last designs for the GNR. The first Yorkshire Engine Co. engine was delivered on 29 December 1866, only three days before Sturrock's retirement. The remaining two Yorkshire Engine Co. engines followed in January and February 1867 (YE1–3).[7] Subsequently converted to singles by Patrick Stirling, the three Yorkshire Engine Co. engines were withdrawn between December 1898 and May 1902 after over thirty

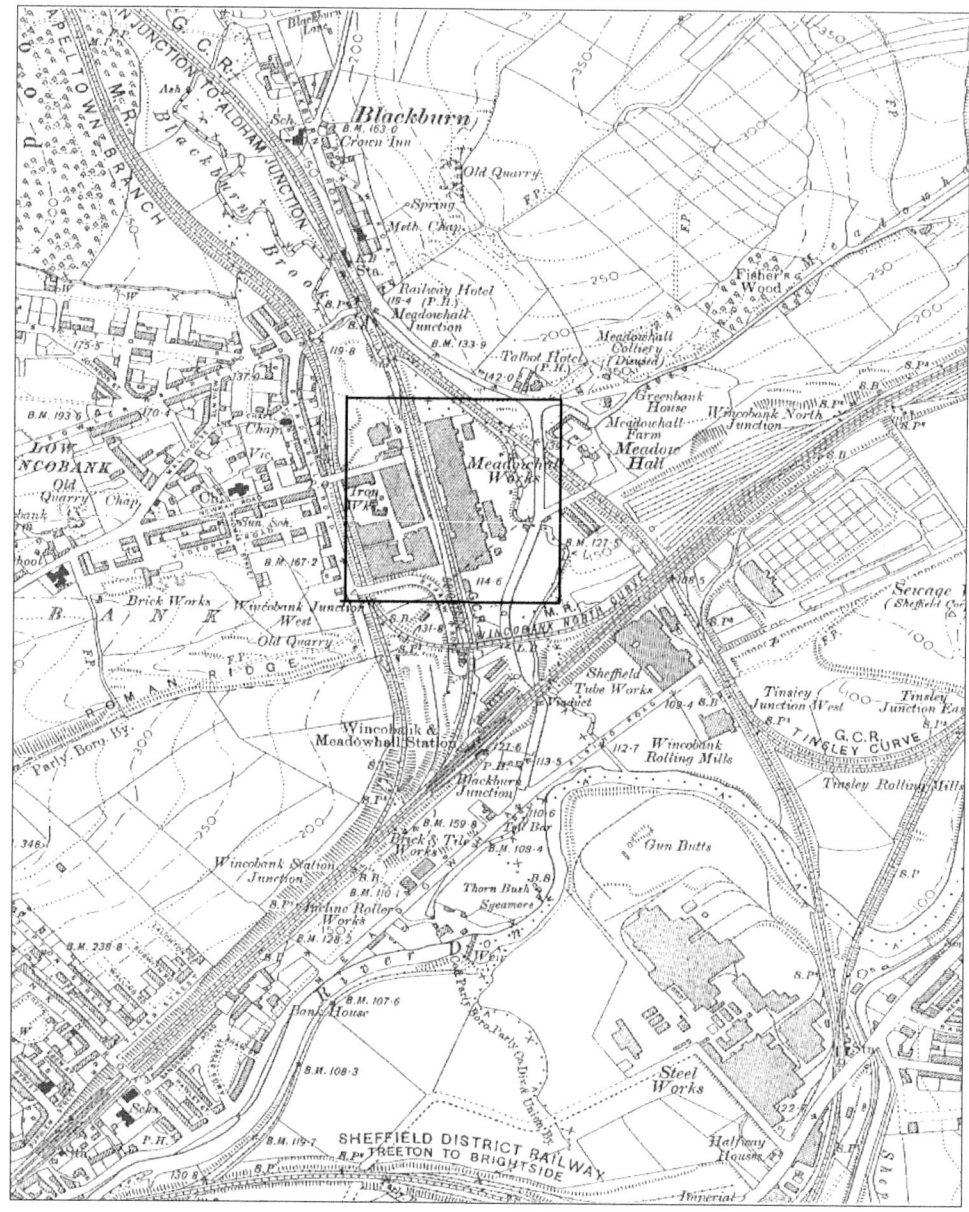

The 1906 Ordnance Survey map shows the Meadowhall works still largely in open country and set amidst a triangle of three railway lines. The section of the Great Central line regularly used for testing locomotives is clearly seen to the west of the works. (Ordnance Survey)

Interior of Meadowhall works, undated. (Sheffield Archives)

years' service. This first Yorkshire Engine Co. order was not profitable; costs were increased because the works was incomplete.[8]

Stirling was content with the quality of the Yorkshire Engine Co.'s workmanship, for the GNR board placed a further order for ten of Stirling's first four-wheeled coupled passenger engines with the Yorkshire Engine Co. in March 1867 (YE54–63). The order was shared between Avonside and the Yorkshire Engine Co. and was won in open competition from thirty manufacturers. The twenty engines of Stirling's 280 series had 6ft 7in driving wheels and 4ft 1in leading wheels.[9] Once again the Yorkshire Engine Co. had to reduce its price to match the £2,370 proposed by Avonside. Delivery of the Yorkshire Engine Co. engines was to commence in April 1868 at a rate of three per month, with the tenth locomotive to be delivered in July 1868. In practice the first locomotive was not delivered till June 1868 and the final engine in March 1869.

The Yorkshire Engine Co. made no more locomotives for the GNR. In common with many other major railways, Stirling took locomotive manufacture in-house. Between 1868 and 1875, all GNR locomotives were built at Doncaster. Like its competitors, the Yorkshire Engine Co. had to look abroad for many of its orders.

When Sturrock took up the Chairmanship in January 1867, he must have been cautiously hopeful for the future. He had an able team of former apprentices around him. As well as Alfred Sacré in the Managing Director post, he could call on Charles Sacré, who had been very supportive over the steam tenders.[10] Edward Sacré in London should bring some commercial expertise to the management team. Robert Hampson, who he also knew well, was in the key role of Works Manager.

Work-in-hand in January 1867 looked encouraging. An order for thirty 0-6-0s had been secured from the East Indian Railway (EIR) in May 1866 (YE4–33) and an order for twenty 0-6-0s had been received from the Great Indian Peninsula Railway (GIPR) two months later (YE34–53). Both were established

*GNR 267–269 (YE1–3) were Sturrock's last 2-4-0s and Yorkshire Engine Co.'s first order. Three were built by Yorkshire Engine and three by John Fowler of Leeds. (*Engineer*)*

5ft 6in-gauge lines. The EIR operated over 1,000 miles of line from Calcutta to Delhi. The GIPR ran for 700 miles from Bombay towards the Ganges plain. Both lines were British-owned companies, with shareholders receiving a Government-guaranteed 5 per cent return.

As 1867 progressed, the market fell away and the Yorkshire Engine Co. became desperate for orders. Some shareholders were already disgruntled. W.W. Hulse, an early investor and partner with his cousin James Whitworth in the Manchester firm of tool makers, sold out in January 1867. Other shareholders objected to calls being made earlier than promised. Hampson, who had his pay increased to £350 a year, ran the works to leave Alfred Sacré free to seek customers, a skill for which he had little training.

Only twenty-four locomotives were ordered in 1867. The GNR order for ten 2-4-0s in February was followed by an order in June from Fairbairns for four 0-6-0s (YE64–67). The year ended with an encouraging order for ten 0-6-0s from the Midland (YE68–77). In spite of hard work involving both Edward and Alfred Sacré and Sturrock to agree payment terms, a tender for fifty locomotives for the Grand Trunk of Canada was lost due to price. Alfred Sacré wrote 'in consequence of slackness at many loco works, prices are low and orders taken at prices which leave no profit'.[11]

Alfred Sacré made every effort to keep his workforce in place. Cast steel tyres were turned; locomotive crank axles were planed and drilled; twenty armour plated shields were produced for the Government. Fifty lamp posts and fifty lamp tops were made for the Chief Constable of Sheffield. An order for 10,000 safes was taken to keep the boiler shop busy. In January 1868 wages were reduced and in March the shareholders were advised there would be no dividend, as the Yorkshire Engine Co. had incurred a loss of £1,054 16s. By June Hampson, the Works Manager, and the Secretary had been given notice, although the former never left.

Alfred Sacré knew that many leading UK locomotive manufacturers were supplying Russian railways, including Beyer Peacock, Dubs, Kitson, Neilson, Sharp Stewart and Robert Stephenson. The Yorkshire Engine Co. would have to look to Russia for orders. Skilled men and workshops would be required to complete assembly locally. Payment arrangements would be complex.

Between June 1868 and June 1870 the Yorkshire Engine Co. obtained eighty-three orders for locomotives. Of these, fifty-eight, or almost 70 per cent of the Yorkshire Engine Co.'s orders, were placed by three Russian railways. The Yorkshire Engine Co.'s first Russian customer in August 1868 was the Tambov-Koslov, which was to open in 1869 and subsequently became part of the Ryazan-Uralsk Railway. An order was placed for eight 0-6-0s and four 2-4-0s for delivery in early 1869 (YE80–91). In subsequent years the Yorkshire Engine Co. also supplied large quantities of spares to the Tambov-Koslov and to the

GNR 269 (YE3) is shown late in its life following modification by Stirling to 2-2-2, as Sturrock had originally planned. (Great Northern Railway Society)

GNR No. 294 (YE58) towards the end of its days; it was one of ten 2-4-0s built by the Yorkshire Engine Co. in 1868 for Patrick Stirling, Sturrock's successor as Locomotive Superintendent of the GNR. (Great Northern Railway Society)

Moscow-Kursk, which had the same president as the Tambov-Koslov. The order was despatched in April 1869 and part payment received. Although the engines performed well, £11,709 10s was still outstanding in January 1870 and the Yorkshire Engine Co. overdraft uncomfortably high.

The Yorkshire Engine Co.'s largest Russian customer was the Poti-Tiflis Railway. Built initially for strategic reasons, the railway was to run from the small port of Poti on the Black Sea to Baku on the Caspian Sea. The first 169-mile section of 5ft-gauge line ran from Poti to Tiflis, now Tbilisi, the capital of Georgia. It was constructed by French/British-owned firm of contractors using soldiers from a Russian railway battalion. A total of thirty-eight locomotives were supplied over a two-year period and orders were received for spares in subsequent years.

The third Russian customer was the Moscow-Ryazan Railway. Largely financed by a railway speculator using German money, the line was one of the few to prosper in the 1860s. Eight 0-6-0s were ordered in July 1869 (YE121–128).

The Yorkshire Engine Co.'s first major overseas order (YE4–33) was for 30 0-6-0s in May 1866 for the East Indian Railway. (Sheffield Archives)

To develop its Russian business, the Yorkshire Engine Co. appointed George Payne Kitson and John Arthur Wright as agents in St Petersburg. To facilitate the signing of contracts, Wright was given power of attorney.[12] Alfred Sacré visited St Petersburg. It was agreed that Kitson and Wright should represent three UK firms of the Yorkshire Engine Co., Cammell & Co., who were to be a major Yorkshire Engine Co. customer, and Gloucester Wagon. Each firm would pay a quarterly retainer of £250 to be recovered from commission on orders. Land was acquired in St Petersburg to be used to assemble engines.

Even before a formal agreement had been signed with the Russian agents, problems arose. Using his power of attorney, Wright had signed the Moscow-Ryazan contract in July 1869 with a penalty clause of £3,500 if the engines were not delivered by 31 December 1869. Even worse, the engines could be rejected if not delivered on time. Wright defended his action to the Yorkshire Engine Co. board by stating Kitsons had accepted an order on worse terms and that the Yorkshire Engine Co. would not have obtained the order if Wright had not agreed to the penalties.

By November 1869 it was clear the order would not be delivered on time. The board learnt that Kitsons were also behind and that penalties were likely to be imposed, because the railway was losing business due to locomotive shortages. The issue was discussed with Sturrock and the board declined to despatch the engines in case they were rejected for late delivery. The locomotives were eventually despatched in February, when Kitson & Wright assured the board the locomotives would be accepted or they would find other buyers. By April the locomotives were being erected at the port of Pillau in East Prussia. Pillau is now in the Kaliningrad, then Konigsberg, area of Russia, north of the modern Polish border and south of Lithuania, several hundred miles from the locomotives' ultimate destination.[13]

The largest overseas order was placed by the Poti-Tiflis Railway. The first two contracts for supplying twenty locomotives were signed in Paris in December 1868. The contractors, Crawley & Meynier, agreed to provide a jetty and unloading facilities at Poti. The Yorkshire Engine Co. was required to accept a second order the following year for a further eighteen locomotives at a lower price.

The locomotives were to be designed by the Yorkshire Engine Co. The initial order was for ten 0-6-4Ts for goods traffic and ten 0-4-4Ts for passenger work, an unusual choice in both instances. Articulated 0-6-4Ts had been used in France, Austria and Switzerland since the 1850s, but the rigid form adopted for the Poti-Tiflis was uncommon. 0-4-4Ts had appeared in the UK on the South Eastern in 1866 and in the USA. The Poti-Tiflis locomotives were at the forefront of new design.[14]

One of eight 0-6-0s (YE121–8) built for the Moscow Ryazan Railway in 1870 to 5ft gauge. (Sheffield Archives)

It is not clear whether this was inspired by the contractors or by Sturrock's liking for innovation. The drawings in the Yorkshire Engine Co. archive are signed off by Sturrock's son Gordon, suggesting Sturrock himself may have been involved.

The first eight engines were loaded on ship for delivery to Poti in August 1869. The second order for fifteen more 0-6-4Ts and three more 0-4-4Ts was received the following month (YE132–149). Sturrock advised the board the contractors wanted some modifications to the design. The board agreed, provided Crawley & Meynier paid the extra cost.

When the first shipment reached Poti, the pier was found to be non-existent. The Yorkshire Engine Co.'s man on the spot found Poti teeming with snakes, lizards and jackals. One engine landed in the mud as a result of a storm and the ship took the rest of the consignment back to Constantinople. Sturrock advised the shareholders that the Yorkshire Engine Co. should not ultimately be out of pocket, but there looked to be scope for a long drawn-out lawsuit involving both the contractors and the shipper. Solicitors were consulted.

Hampson was sent out to Poti in January 1870 to get the first six locomotives assembled to the client's satisfaction. Due to fever amongst the workforce, all the locomotives were not completed till January 1871, when 80 per cent of the money owed was paid. However the Yorkshire Engine Co.'s claim for extra costs of £7,412 for modifications to all thirty-eight engines was still being pursued by Edward and Charles Sacré in November 1872. The dispute with the shipper also continued for many years. In spite of the problems already encountered, the Yorkshire Engine Co. provided large quantities of spare parts, including tyres and fireboxes, to the Poti-Tiflis in subsequent years.

The company was now showing a profit, but running out of cash. The accounts recorded a profit of £3,455 after depreciation in the year to March 1869. A profit of £3,179 was shown in the following year, but there was no cash to pay the promised dividend of 2.5 per cent. Due to the failure of its Russian customers to pay up and the extra costs of shipping and erecting locomotives in Russia, the overdraft limit of £30,000 had been reached. Sturrock went to the Sheffield & Rotherham Bank in May 1870 to ask for an extension to the overdraft. The bank agreed £35,000 for six weeks, but required the overdraft to be reduced to £20,000 in six months. The board would have either to call for an additional £5 per share from shareholders or raise a mortgage, if it was to continue in business.

Poti-Tiflis (later Transcaucasian Railway) 0-6-4T, one of twenty-five built by the Yorkshire Engine Co. in two batches in 1869 and 1870, for the line which ran from the Black Sea to the town now called Tiblisi (YE98–107 and 132–146). (Finnish Railway Museum)

British-owned South American Railways were an important market for the Yorkshire Engine Co. The first South American customer was the Buenos Ayres Great Southern, which acquired the first three of several batches of 4-4-0s in 1870 (YE130). (Derek Penney Collection)

YE169 was one of four 2-4-0Ts supplied to the 5ft 6in-gauge Buenos Ayres Great Southern in 1871. (Derek Penney Collection)

YE164 was supplied to the 3ft 6in-gauge Imperial Japanese Railways in 1870 and was the only locomotive supplied by the Yorkshire Engine Co. to Japan. (Peter Hawkins Collection)

YE164 survives as a static exhibit at the Oume Railway Park in 2008; it ceased to work in 1918 and was designated a Japanese railway cultural asset in 1961. (Eiji Nozawa)

Sturrock decided the responsibilities of the Chairman position were not enjoyable. He tendered his resignation to the board on 27 May 1870. He agreed to stay on as a director. The cash position continued to deteriorate. £22,000 was owed on Russian contracts in July and the overdraft was still above £28,000. Alfred Sacré prepared a cash flow forecast, assuming no remittances from Russia, and went with Barker, the acting Chairman, and another director, Lees, to ask the bank for help. A temporary overdraft of £31,344 was agreed, but the limit was reduced to £20,000 by the year end, a modest easing of the deal agreed with Sturrock.

To maintain confidence between the board and the shareholders, the board agreed to ask for an independent report on the company from W.W. Hulse, a former shareholder and at one time managing partner of Whitworths the tool makers. Hulse was now an independent consultant. He reported in February 1871, accusing the board of 'mismanagement and waste of economy'. He wanted to abolish the post of Managing Director and suggested all work not directly concerned with locomotive manufacture and repair should cease. He stated the buildings were overvalued in the balance sheet and recommended the board should be replaced. He suggested raising funds through preference shares with 5 per cent interest.

Barker refuted the recommendations one by one. Hulse's credibility was not helped by erroneous profit figures in his report. Barker supported the Managing Director role. He thought ordinary shares would be cheaper than preference shares. He did not agree with abandoning other engineering work which could enable the machinery to be used profitably. Sturrock supported Barker and suggested the total loss of £1,628 in four years was hardly mismanagement. Avonside had lost £8,000 in one year and £4,000 in another. Material costs were low and prices kept down by competition.

Barker, Eden, Sturrock and the other directors resigned. Alfred Sacré told the board he was joining Avonside at the end of March, since his five-year contract had not been renewed. A shareholders' consultation committee was appointed to work with the new board.

By the following month the new board realised they could not cope without the experience of the former directors. Barker, Eden (now Lord Auckland) and Sturrock were reappointed. Hampson was promoted to Manager on £400 per year plus a bonus. Charles Sacré continued as a shareholder representative. The appointment of a Managing Director or General Manager was deferred. The accounts to March 1871 showed a loss of £11,621 13s with £17,200 still owed on the Russian contracts.

In May 1871 Sturrock sold his shares and resigned. The Chairman advised the AGM that Sturrock wished 'to be relieved of any further trouble' and 'to leave himself leisure for more congenial pursuits'.[15] Lord Auckland also resigned. Both suffered a substantial loss on their shares. The new board concluded that the business could not justify a General Manager or Managing Director. Edward Sacré and his firm of Hunt & Sacré were employed to run the business on a commission of 1 per cent per cent of turnover plus 5 per cent of profits after payment of dividend.

By the end of 1871, after around five years trading, the Yorkshire Engine Co. had delivered 169 locomotives or an average of thirty-four locomotives a year. It had achieved a reasonable spread of customers, but was only keeping its machinery and workforce occupied by taking on general engineering work, a pattern which was to persist throughout its existence. In addition to overseas orders from Russian and Indian railways, the company had made its first deliveries to South America, where the Buenos Ayres Great Southern had acquired three 4-4-0s in 1870 (YE129–131) and four 2-4-0Ts in 1871 (YE166–169). One of the 2-4-0Ts survives on a plinth in San Rafael, Mendoza in Argentina.

The Victorian Railways in Australia had bought six 0-6-0s (YE153–158) and the Japanese Government Railway a single 2-4-0T (YE164). The locomotive was used initially on the first 3ft 6in-gauge line from Shinbashi to Yokohama and subsequently for ballasting work. Withdrawn in 1918, the locomotive has been preserved and is now on display as a stationary exhibit at the Oume Railway Park in Tokyo.[16] The Yorkshire Engine Co. never supplied another locomotive to Japan, although spares were provided shortly after delivery.

At home orders from the Great Northern and Midland had been supplemented with sales to three smaller railways and to the first industrial customers. The Yorkshire Engine Co. supplied the Midland with ten Kirtley-designed Class 480 0-6-0s in 1868–9 (YE68–77), part of a total order for 232 locomotives

One of three 0-4-0STs built for Earl Fitzwilliam's collieries in 1869, the Yorkshire Engine Co.'s first venture into industrial locomotives. (Sheffield Archives)

spread between five outside manufacturers and the Midland itself.[17] The Belfast, Holywood & Bangor bought two 2-4-0Ts (YE 151–2) and the Monmouthshire two 0-6-0Ts (YE159–60). The first industrial customer was Earl Fitzwilliam in 1869 with three 0-4-0STs *Victoria, Milton* and *Wentworth* (YE118–120). Other industrial customers for small saddle tanks were Kiveton Park Colliery, Wingerworth Iron (YE162–3) and Darfield Main Colliery (YE165). Charles Cammell was the largest customer for general and railway-related engineering work. Locomotive repairs were being undertaken on locomotives manufactured by other companies and the spares business was developing. However, cash was short and prices low.

Notes

1. PRO Rail 1008/1, 23 July 1864.
2. John Tomlinson, *Stories and Sketches relating to Yorkshire* (1868), pp.208–210.
3. 30 May 1867 AGM.
4. Board minute, 4 July 1867.
5. PRO Rail 236/33, 14 November 1865.
6. PRO Rail 236/208, 22 February 1866.
7. N. Groves *GNR Locomotive History volume 1*, pp.119–122.
8. Shareholder meeting, July 1868.
9. Groves Volume 2, pp.8–11.
10. *Backtrack,* February 2005.
11. Board minute, 8 August 1867.
12. Board minute, 17 September 1868.
13. Board minute, 13 April 1870.
14. R.A.S. Hennessey, *Transcaucasian Railway* (2004), pp.17–19.
15. Board minute, 24 May 1871, and report of shareholders' meeting, 17 June 1871.
16. Locomotive History Society of Japan, *Cavalcade of Japanese Locomotives* (1986).
17. *Locomotive Magazine*, October 1907 and April 1937.

2

Experiments and Failure
1872–1883

In February 1872 the board agreed to replace Hunt & Sacré's initial one-year contract for managing the business with a seven-year agreement to pay the firm 1 per cent of turnover plus 5 per cent of profits after dividend. Edward Sacré would attend all board meetings. R.S. Hampson would have day-to-day management responsibility. He was receiving a salary of £400 a year, which was increased to £500 a year in February 1873. In addition Hampson was awarded the sum of £20 for every 1 per cent of dividend paid to the shareholders.

The Yorkshire Engine Co.'s financial position was improving; at the March 1872 annual meeting the Chairman reported a gross profit of £1,183. After depreciation and write-offs, the loss for the year was £1,244, a substantial recovery from the two previous years, when losses of £11,621 and £7,286 were reported. The Chairman advised the shareholders that the order book stood at £140,000, including orders for £90,000 of locomotives for Mexican, Spanish, Belgian and UK railways. The workforce had increased from around 300 to over 600 men.

Edward Sacré perceived he had two major tasks. He needed to strengthen the company's cash position by recovering the £17,000 owed on the various Russian contracts. He also needed to broaden the company's range of products. To this end he introduced the Yorkshire Engine Co. to two entrepreneurial engineers, Robert Fairlie and Loftus Perkins. In October 1871 he told the board that he had been talking to Robert Fairlie about manufacturing his patent locomotives for a 5 per cent royalty. In November he reported on conversations with Loftus Perkins about building marine and traction engines to Loftus Perkins' patents. The Chairman was cautious about the link with Perkins, following discussions with a Col. Anderson, who had suggested the venture was too costly for a company of the Yorkshire Engine Co.'s size. When Sacré suggested to the board that a sample marine engine could be built for £4,000, the board agreed to proceed.

Robert Fairlie was born in 1831 and received his training at Swindon and Crewe. After serving as Engineer and Manager of the Londonderry & Coleraine Railway and a period with the Bombay & Baroda Railway, he returned to England to concentrate on developing his articulated steam locomotive patent. Fairlie's original patent of 1864 had a single firebox and central chimney. A similar locomotive had been built by John Cockerill of the Seraing works in Belgium for the Semmering incline in Austria in 1851. Whether or not Fairlie knew of the Seraing machine, Fairlie's modified designs from 1868 onwards closely matched the Seraing locomotive.[1]

How and why the Yorkshire Engine Co. became involved with Fairlie is not clear. The early Fairlie locomotives were built by James Cross & Co. of St Helens and then for a short period from 1869–70 by Fairlie himself in a joint venture with George England junior at the Hatcham ironworks at New Cross in London. This venture collapsed and Fairlie arranged for Sharp Stewart and Avonside to build locomotives to his design. Their first Fairlies were completed in 1870 and 1871 respectively.

It seems possible that the Yorkshire Engine Co. became involved as a result of an introduction from Alfred Sacré, who was now running Avonside. Alfred may have suggested to Fairlie that he should contact his brother Edward to see if the Yorkshire Engine Co. could help with modifying three Fairlie locomotives

One of five Fairlie 0-6-6-0s built by the Yorkshire Engine Co. in 1872 for the Mexican Railway, these were the first Fairlies built by the Yorkshire Engine Co. (YE170–174). (Sheffield Archives)

built to a design by Douglas Fox for the Southern & Western Railway of Queensland. These locomotives were built without input from Fairlie himself. After two of the three locomotives had been tried in Australia in early 1867 and found wanting, all three were shipped back to England. Fairlie, concerned for his reputation, acquired the locomotives and had them modified and converted to standard gauge. Two of the three went to the Central Railway of Uruguay and one, *Victoria*, to the Bury Port & Gwendraeth Railway in South Wales.[2] The Yorkshire Engine Co. produced a range of parts for Robert Fairlie for the Bury Port locomotive in September 1873, including piston rods and name plates. The Yorkshire Engine Co. may have undertaken the modifications, but the order is not recorded in the order book. The two locomotives acquired by the Central Railway of Uruguay are shown in the railway company's records as built by the Yorkshire Engine Co. and they produced axles, tyres, brake blocks, gauges and other spares for the Central Uruguay in January 1875.[3]

The Mexican Railway was the first and largest customer for Yorkshire Engine Co.-built Fairlie locomotives. The first of three orders for a total of thirteen 0-6-6-0s was received in October 1871 via G.B. Crawley, the engineer with whom the Yorkshire Engine Co. had had dealings on the Poti-Tiflis contracts and with whom the company was still in dispute about additional payments. The initial order was for five standard-gauge locomotives (YE170–174) for delivery in 1872. A further five were ordered for delivery in 1873 (YE190–194). The wheels were 3ft 6in in diameter and the total heating surface 1,688 sq. ft. The locomotives had to be capable of burning both coal and wood, since both fuels were used on the line. In 1883 three more Fairlies were supplied to the Mexican Railway (YE365–367). These had 3ft 9in wheels and larger cylinders and fuel bunkers. Walschaerts valve gear was probably used for the first time in the UK on the 1873 batch of Fairlies, but was replaced by Allan straight link motion on the third batch.[4]

During the period 1872-4 the Yorkshire Engine Co. built its first Fairlie locomotive for the Nitrate Railways of South America (YE175). It was a 0-6-6-0 and was delivered in 1874. Orders for Fairlies were also received from Sweden, Belgium and Brazil. It is not clear to what extent Fairlie had an input into the design of these locomotives. Fairlie had an office in London and may well have contributed to the general design, leaving the Yorkshire Engine Co. to produce the main drawings, many of which survive in the Sheffield archives.[5]

The three locomotives for Brazil and Sweden were 0-4-4-0s. One (YE178) was sent to Rio de Janeiro in 1873 for the 3ft 7¼in Canto-Gallo Railway. Two (YE176–177) went to the standard-gauge

The third batch of three Fairlie 0-6-6-0s delivered in 1883 to the Mexican Railway (YE365–7). (LM p.21)

One of the two 0-4-4-0 Fairlies built by the Yorkshire Engine Co. for the Hallsberg Motala Mjolby Railway in Sweden at Skanninge Station (YE176–177). (Swedish Railway Museum)

Hallsberg-Motola-Mjobly line in Sweden in 1874. These locomotives, named *Berserk* and *Nidhogg*, were designed to burn peat. Used mainly for goods traffic, they were not a great success and were rebuilt in 1887 as four small 0-4-2STs. They were finally withdrawn between 1899 and 1908.[6]

The Fairlie locomotive for the standard-gauge Grand Compagnie du Luxembourg (YE212) was a 0-6-6-0 and was the only example of its type in Belgium. It was named *Fenton* after a Mr W. Fenton of Rochdale who was president of the Board of Directors and it weighed 64 tons. When the Luxembourg company was taken over by Belgian State Railway in 1878 it was numbered 969 and used principally for hauling local goods trains in the Brussels area. It was scrapped in 1887. The Yorkshire Engine Co. also supplied six 0-6-0s (YE213–218) to the Luxembourg company in 1873.

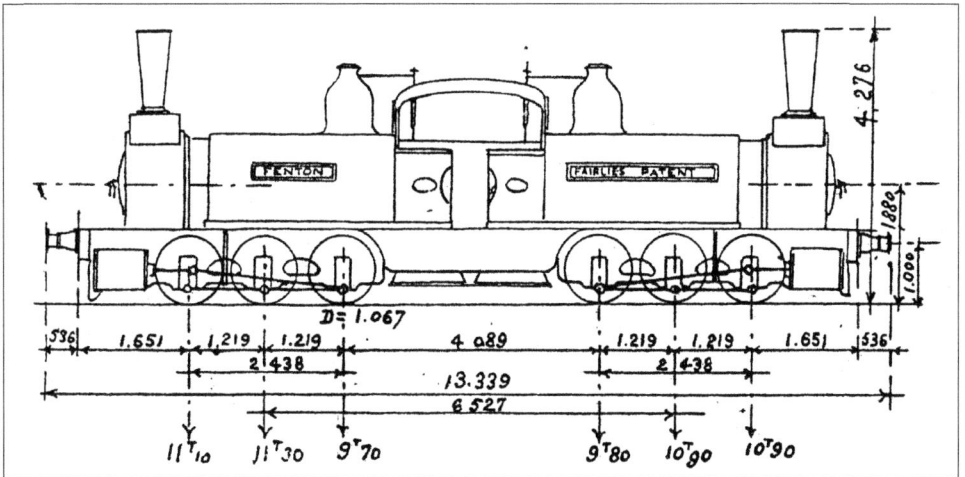

YE212 Fenton, a 0-6-6-0 Fairlie for the UK-owned Luxembourg Railway, of 1872. (Locomotive, December 1929)

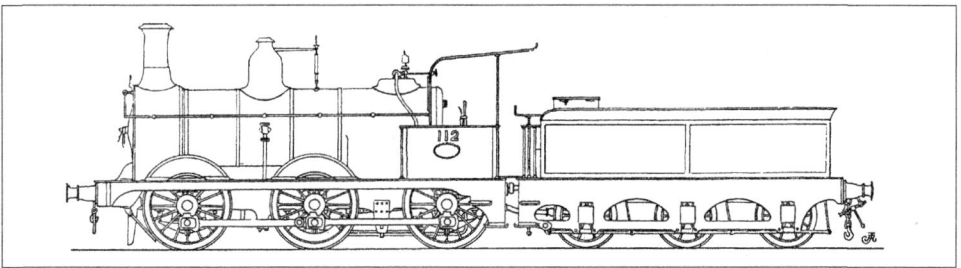

Luxembourg Railway's 0-6-0 goods locomotive No. 112 (YE216) of 1873 as originally built. (Locomotive, April 1929)

Numbered 963–968 after the takeover, most were withdrawn by 1904 except 964, which remained in service until 1913. The 0-6-0s were similar to Johnson's 0-6-0s built by the Yorkshire Engine Co. for the Great Eastern in 1872–3 (YE195–209).[7]

In February 1873 the Yorkshire Engine Co. board was advised that ten Fairlie engines were to be built for Peru (YE219–228). One third of the ultimate cost was to be paid on production of the drawings, 80 per cent of the balance on completion of the engines at the works and the remainder on delivery. The order was placed by Montero Bros of Lima on behalf of the General South American Co. In July 1868 Montero Bros had obtained a concession from the Peruvian Government to build a railway inland from the port of Iquique; a second concession to build a railway from the port of Pisagua was granted to them in May 1869. Both railways were designed principally to transport nitrates.[8] The railways had been built in an area which is now in northern Chile but was then under Peruvian control. Nitrates are found on a narrow strip of desert set on a high plateau running parallel to the coast for about 500 miles from Pisagua in the north to Taltal in Chile in the south.

The Montero's railways did not prosper. In July 1874 the Yorkshire Engine Co. board received a request from Fairlie to suspend all work on the Montero engines. At this time the Montero's railways were being reorganised and a new company was being formed to take over the concessions. The company was to be called the National Nitrates Railway Co. of Peru, in which the Montero Bros retained a major stake.[9] However, Fairlie appears not to have told the Yorkshire Engine Co. board the full story. The board was, therefore, unwilling to comply with the request to suspend work.

By January 1875 the first five engines were complete but the General South American Co. refused to pay 80 per cent of the balance due. The ultimate customer for the ten engines must be presumed to be the new National Nitrates Railway Co. of Peru, although the contract had been placed before the company took over the Montero's concessions. As the General South American Co.'s customer was unable or unwilling to complete the purchase, the Yorkshire Engine Co. had to consider what to do with the locomotives.

The Yorkshire Engine Co. records are imprecise with regard to the disposal of the engines built under this contract. It would appear that four and possibly five of the locomotives completed by January 1875 (YE 219–223) were shipped to the Poti-Tiflis Railway, subsequently known as the Transcaucasian Railway. A visitor to the railway noted that the Fairlies, of which there were forty-five on the line from various makers by 1909, could handle thirteen goods or seventeen passenger vehicles up and down the steep inclines of the Suram pass.[10] Fitted with suitable axles for the 5ft gauge and weighing 77 tons in working order, the locomotives had a working pressure of 160psi. Only four Yorkshire Engine Co. Fairlies are recorded in the Poti-Tiflis Railway's records and it has not been conclusively established what happened to the fifth. It seems possible that this 'lost' locomotive (probably Yorkshire Engine Co. 219) was sent to Pisagua in spite of the request from the Monteros to suspend the order. Both Dewhurst and Abbot, who wrote extensively on the Fairlie locomotive in the 1960s, indicate that the Nitrate Railways had at least one more Yorkshire Engine Co. Fairlie than is recorded in Yorkshire Engine Co. records, but their lists do not record a Yorkshire Engine Co. works number for the additional engine. The recent book by Donald Binns on the Nitrate Railways Co. also concludes that one engine out of the initial batch of five must have been delivered to Pisagua.[11]

The second batch of five Fairlies from the Montero order (YE 224–228) seem to have been completed and remained in the yard at Meadowhall. One of the five locomotives was hired out to the East & West Junction Railway during 1876–7 for a period of about twelve months till passenger services were suspended. The East & West Junction was a cross-country line linking Stratford with Evesham in the west and with Towcester, Northampton and Bedford in the east. The locomotive is similar in appearance to those shipped to Poti.[12] An advertisement offering for sale five new Fairlie locomotives built by the Yorkshire Engine Co. appeared in the *Engineer* for 16 August 1878, even though one of the five locomotives was not new and had been used on the East & West Junction. Eventually in 1882 the locomotives were shipped to their original destination. They were bought by a new Nitrate Railways Co., an English company which had in that year taken over the railways once owned by the Monteros.

Before the locomotives were shipped out to a part of Peru, in an area now part of Chile, modifications were made. A Bissell truck was added at the outer end of both bogies. This increased the weight of the locomotives to around 85 tons in working order. According to a report in *Engineering* dated 7 August 1885 they were the heaviest locomotives in the world. Robert Fairlie visited the Meadowhall works in September 1881 to check on the changes being made.[13] He had one of the five engines stripped down for detailed examination. This might well have been the engine which had been used on the East & West Junction and was not new, as the advertisement had implied.

If the link with Fairlie led to useful and potentially profitable business, the same can not be said for the relationship with Loftus Perkins. Perkins was an engineer and inventor. Born in 1834, he joined his father's business in London before spending a year in New York at the age of twenty. He returned to work again for his father before moving to Germany, where he developed and installed heating systems for buildings. When he made contact with the Yorkshire Engine Co. he was back working in partnership with his father and had already registered many patents for steam boilers, steam engines and machinery for propelling vessels.

At the time of his discussions with Edward Sacré in 1871 Perkins had just built a three-wheeled 'road locomotive'. The vehicle had a boiler which was said to operate at 450psi. The front wheel, which both drove and steered the machine, was 2ft in diameter with a rubber tyre. According to Fletcher's book *Steam Locomotion on Common Roads* of 1891, the vehicle 'was for some time used by the Yorkshire Engine Co., Meadow Hall Works, Sheffield'. Maybe it was taken to Meadowhall to convince the Yorkshire Engine

One of five Fairlie 2-6-6-2s sent to Nitrate Railways in 1882; the locomotives were built as 0-6-6-0s in 1874 and remained in the yard at Meadowhall. They were modified by Fairlie, who added a Bissell truck at both ends. (Derek Penney Collection)

Co. board of the soundness of Perkins's steam engine designs. The Yorkshire Engine Co. board records show a traction engine was tested at the works in November 1872. The vehicle was capable of 8mph and almost noiseless. Edward Sacré had a keen interest in locomotives on roads and appeared before a House of Commons Select Committee of July 1873, which looked into the possibility of lifting some of the restrictions which then applied to such vehicles. The restrictions were not lifted and the requirement for a man to walk in front of the vehicle continued to apply.

In June 1872 Edward Sacré advised the board that he wished to build a 500hp marine engine to Perkins design at a cost of £5,000. The board were unwilling to proceed since no customer had been identified. Sacré brought the matter up again at the next meeting and suggested making a 250hp engine, but the board was still reluctant. Advertisements were placed in the *Engineer* to try and attract customers. To get things moving, Perkins suggested building a 120hp engine and an order for a 120hp Marine Engine is recorded on 24 August 1872. By October Edward had spoken to his brother Charles Sacré about a 130hp marine engine for one of the MSLR's ships and with Messrs Wilson for an 80hp engine. £4,500 was approved for spending on two marine engines. The sales appear to have gone ahead, since the board noted in May 1874 that there had been a loss of £3,000 on the first Perkins' engines.

The Yorkshire Engine Co. had been placed on the Admiralty list of approved suppliers and in February 1873 the Admiralty expressed interest in a marine engine. A trial was organised with senior Naval officers and the Duke of Edinburgh present. Eighteen months later the company was asked to tender by the Admiralty for 900hp engines for a vessel called the *Pelican*. The contract was agreed in December 1874 for a price of £12,250.

By March 1875 Perkins advised the Yorkshire Engine Co. he was considering licensing his patent to others, as he was still dissatisfied with progress; in April Perkins arranged for the Thames Iron Works to have a sublicense. Matters for the Yorkshire Engine Co., however, became significantly worse. The purchaser of a 250hp engine lost confidence in the design and withdrew; Perkins sued the Yorkshire Engine Co. for not making sufficient checks before accepting the order. As a consequence of the lawsuit, the Admiralty also lost confidence and withdrew its order for engines for the Pelican. By the year to March 1877 losses of £34,531 15s 4d had been incurred on Perkins engines, of which sum about £8,000

This tram was ordered by the Belgian Street Railway in 1873 and was built to a Loftus Perkins patent with a boiler pressure of 500psi. (Sheffield Archives)

related to legal charges for the lawsuit. As the Chairman's adviser had suggested, the whole marine engine project had been too large and too risky for the Yorkshire Engine Co.

A second venture on which Edward Sacré and Loftus Perkins risked the Yorkshire Engine Co. shareholders' money was the construction of tramway engines. The Yorkshire Engine Co. received an order from T. Vaucamps of Belgium on 9 October 1873 for 'one tramway locomotive on Perkins's patent principle to tracing submitted.'[14] The locomotive was to be ready in two months. Duplicate items for this tramway engine were ordered in April 1874. These included an axle, oil box, piston rings and pumps.[15] The engine was constructed at Meadowhall to Loftus Perkins patented water tube system. The wrought-iron tubes had an internal diameter of 2 ¾in and were 3/8in thick. The tubes were proved to a pressure of 2,500psi and the engine worked to a pressure of 500psi. It was tried out on the adjacent MS&LR line and achieved speeds up to 15mph on gradients from 1:200 to 1:80. The initial reports from Belgium were favourable, where it drew a one-horse passenger car. By 1875 doubts had set in and, according to D.K. Clark, M. Vaucamps of the Belgian Street Railway modified the cylinders and introduced a new system of gearing, which proved unsuccessful. The engine was then taken apart and sold for scrap. No works number is recorded for this engine.

No further attempt to enter the tramway engine market was made for three years. However, in March 1878 the board agreed to build a tramway engine to Edward Sacré's drawings.[16] The Chairman told the 1878 annual meeting of shareholders that, if street locomotives came into vogue, the shareholders would make much money. Street locomotives used to replace horses could reduce tramway operating costs by 50 per cent. The directors were shown the tramway engine in operation, but the Chairman made no promise as to the level of future profits. The engine as shown had some faults, but Sacré said these could be easily overcome. The shareholders were encouraging and asked to come to more trials. This engine is listed as YE358.

Edward Sacré's tramway engine is on trial on the Sheffield tramway system in October 1878; Sheffield Corporation did not buy the locomotive and it probably ended its days on the Wigtownshire Railway. (Sheffield Archives)

Although the Swansea tramways had expressed interest earlier in the year, the first trials were on the Birkenhead tramway in August 1878 and proved 'fairly satisfactory'. In October the engine was tried out on the Sheffield tramways and the board was sufficiently encouraged to agree to the construction of a second engine. Hampson, the Manager, had been to Paris to see a tramway engine and was satisfied that the Yorkshire Engine Co. engine was superior. In March 1879 the breakthrough appeared to come when two tramway engines were ordered from Barcelona. It was agreed that Sacré could attend the trials provided his expenses did not exceed £50. Unfortunately he was too ill to attend and Hampson went in his place and reported 'our engine is spoken of as the best engine yet made both as regards appearance and mechanical appliances'. Hampson believed there was good business to be had in Spain and he looked to be right as the Yorkshire Engine Co.'s agents in Spain came forward with an order for four engines at £2,050 each. Unfortunately the agent did not conclude the order and, a year later, in April 1880, the Yorkshire Engine Co. were still trying to obtain payment for the two Barcelona engines.

It would appear that these two engines were ultimately returned to Meadowhall. In February 1883 Thomas Wheatley, who had been Locomotive Superintendent of the North British Railway and was now General Manager of the Wigtownshire Railway, visited the works to see two tramway locomotives. One was in good condition and the other covered in yellow clay, having recently been sent to Belgium and fallen into mud when being transferred on a lighter to or from the port. Wheatley's engine driver, James Pirie, was instructed to clean up the mud-covered engine and take it to Huddersfield on a wagon. Huddersfield had tramlines laid, but was not yet fully operational. Pirie took the engine, a trailer car and some wagons out on the streets of Huddersfield at night. He found the going rough and realised he had run a considerable distance past the end of the rails! He subsequently took Wheatley, his son and a party of Huddersfield councillors on a run through the streets. The engine wheels were rough as a result of the off-rail venture and Pirie arranged to change the wheels. As he was in the process of doing this, he was told Thomas Wheatley had died and was ordered to return to Wigtownshire. Some months later Pirie was sent to a yard in Ashton under Lyne, probably that of Isaac Bolton, where he completed the refurbishment of the engine. Pirie than left for India and it is not clear whether either this engine or the engine seen in good condition at Meadowhall went to the Wigtownshire. However, when the Wigtownshire Railway locomotives were listed in 1885 a tramway engine is shown in the list.[17]

The Yorkshire Engine Co.'s venture into the tramway engine market died with Edward Sacré's departure. Sacré was too ill to continue managing the Yorkshire Engine Co. and handed over his role to

One of twenty-six 0-6-0 metre-gauge F class locomotives for Indian State Railways; these were numbered F21–46 (YE293–318). (LM p.22)

his partner Hunt in October 1879. Edward Sacré died of kidney failure on 26 October 1881 at the age of forty-three. By August 1883 the tramway assets had been realised at a loss of £1,885, a modest sum by comparison with the losses on the Perkins marine engines, but still significant for a small company struggling to survive.

Edward Sacré had not devoted all his time to Fairlie locomotives, marine engines and tramways. During the period from 1872 to 1883 the Yorkshire Engine Co. built a total of 199 locomotives, including the three tramway locomotives. This averages about seventeen locomotives a year, around half the rate achieved in the first five years of trading and well under the original fifty locomotives a year given to investors. The works was underused and overheads too high, even when account is taken of the general engineering work undertaken for local firms. Charles Cammell and John Brown were important customers as well as several of the local collieries for general engineering work. Cammell ordered large quantities of cranks, pistons, wheels, propellers and frames. Duplicate parts for the Yorkshire Engine Co.'s own locomotives and for those made by other manufacturers generated turnover and kept some skilled men employed.

The largest UK customer in the period was the Great Eastern, which acquired fifteen 0-6-0s in 1872–3 to the design of its engineer, Johnson (YE195–209). Manufacture of these engines, which had 5ft 1in driving wheels and boiler pressure of 140psi, was spread amongst Beyer Peacock, Dubs, Nasmyth Wilson and Robert Stephenson as well as the Yorkshire Engine Co. In spite of the size of the order the Yorkshire Engine Co. incurred a loss of £7,000, indicating the difficulty of getting orders at a worthwhile price. The Lancashire & Yorkshire also ordered 12 0-6-0s, which were delivered in 1875–6 (YE263–274).

The Indian subcontinent remained an important market for British manufacturers during this period. The Yorkshire Engine Co. obtained an order for 26 metre-gauge 0-6-0s for the Indian State Railways for delivery in 1876–7 (YE293–318). 1,035 of those F class mixed traffic locomotives were supplied by various manufacturers between 1874 and 1922. East Indian Railways returned with an order for twenty-five 0-6-0s in 1877 (YE331–355).

Orders were obtained from New Zealand for eleven Class F 0-6-0STs in 1874 (YE239–249). Eighty-eight of these engines were built by seven British builders. One of these locomotives continued in service till 1964. Two Yorkshire engine Class Fs are preserved. One (YE244) is normally operational at Western Springs Railway and a second (YE241) is being used for spares at Ferrymead Museum, Christchurch. The Yorkshire Engine Co. also supplied two 0-4-0Ts in 1875 (YE255–6). A total of twelve of these diminutive Class A locomotives were built by several manufacturers for branch line and shunting duties in the

One of a batch of twenty-five 0-6-0s for the 5ft 6in-gauge East Indian Railway delivered in 1877 (YE331–355). (LM p.16)

The Yorkshire Engine Co. built eleven of the New Zealand 3ft 6in-gauge F class 0-6-0s in 1874; a total of eighty-eight were built by seven UK manufacturers (YE239–249). (LM p.31)

F180 (YE244) is preserved at the Western Springs Railway of the Museum of Transport & Technology, New Zealand. (MOTAT)

Canterbury area. Most had been sold by New Zealand Railways by 1905 and adopted by collieries, timber mills and harbours. No further locomotive orders were secured from New Zealand.

Elsewhere abroad, South America was not just a source of orders for Fairlies. The Buenos Ayres Great Southern ordered two 2-4-0Ts in 1872 (YE183–4) and six 4-4-0s in 1874 (YE229–234) and another four in 1875 (YE275–278). The Peruvian Railway acquired two 3ft 6in-gauge 0-4-0STs in 1873 (YE210–211). In Spain there were orders from the Compostelano for four 0-4-0Ts and from the San Juan de Las Abedesas for three 0-8-0s (YE186–189 and 290–292). The latter were part of a class of six locomotives built for shunting duties, some of which were still working on the RENFE in the 1960s.[18] The Imperial Ottoman bought five 0-6-0s for the Mudanya to Bursa line (YE250–254) and Sharp Stewart passed on an order for four 2-6-0Ts for the Nitrate Railways in 1883 (YE368–371).

In the UK the market was becoming tougher and the railway companies were threatening to build locomotives for sale to third parties. The LNWR had supplied eighty-six 0-6-0s to the Lancashire & Yorkshire Railway between 1871 and 1875. The Yorkshire Engine Co. played a leading role in the formation of the Locomotive Manufacturers' Association (LMA) in June 1875. The LMA was founded to protect the interests of the independent builders. The Association succeeded in preventing the LNWR and other railway-owned works from entering the general market for locomotives.[19]

Some smaller UK railways placed orders with the Yorkshire Engine Co. including the Felixstowe Railway & Pier Co. and the Hoylake & Birkenhead Rail & Tramway Co. In 1877 this railway purchased two 2-4-0s of the Yorkshire Engine Co. design named *West Kirby* and *Birkenhead* (YE356-7). They were retained by the railway till its merger with the Wirral in 1891, when they were sold on to a colliery and a chemical company.[20] However, the most regular UK market was industry and, amongst the customers during this period, was the Appleby Iron Works which acquired a 0-4-0ST in 1875 (YE257). The board allowed Sacré to build 0-4-0STs for stock. This kept the skilled workforce together in difficult times and enabled local collieries and engineering works to purchase off the shelf. This practice of building standard industrial locomotives to stock was continued throughout the Yorkshire Engine Co.'s life.

Building locomotives to stock had cash flow implications and the Yorkshire Engine Co. was short of cash. In spite of Scare's efforts and substantial legal fees, the Russian cash was not recovered and the

San Juan de Las Abedesas 0-8-0T Concost No. 7 delivered in 1876 for the 5ft 6in-gauge Spanish railway (YE292). (Derek Penney Collection)

Imperial Ottoman 0-6-0 for the Mudanya-Bursa line in 1874 (YE250–254). (LM p.26)

Birkenhead (YE357) was the second of two 2-4-0Ts supplied to the Hoylake and Birkenhead in 1877. (Derek Penney Collection)

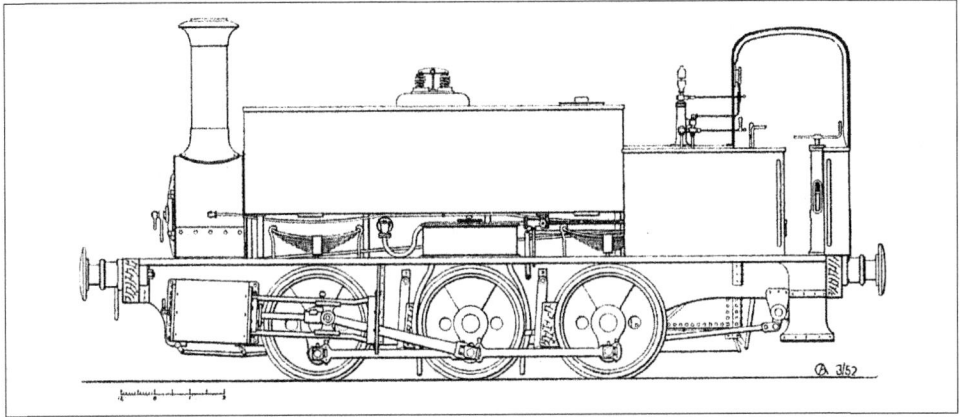

One of three 0-6-0s built for stock in 1878–82 No.325 went to the New Hucknall Colliery and was named No.1 Portland (YE325). (SLS Journal, June 1952)

0-6-0ST Katie (YE282) was built in 1876 and sold to Chatterley Iron; she is shown still operating at Chatterley Whitfield Colliery in 1962. (Alec Swain – Transport Treasury)

Robin Goodfellow (YE361), a diminutive 1ft 8in-gauge coke oven locomotive, was supplied to the Wharncliffe Silkstone Colliery in 1880. (Sheffield Archives)

company continued to operate with a significant overdraft of £20,000 plus. Once the board recognised it would not recover the Russian debts, the company decided to write down the value of its shares by £15 each to cover the loss. A more ingenious method was devised to cover the £34,000 lost on Perkins engines; the board decided to write back around £18,000 of depreciation, a somewhat dubious practice even in those days, in order to leave a smaller loss to carry forward and thus to improve the prospect of paying dividends in the future. Turnover was falling. It had been £81,000 in 1878 but was only £43,000 in 1879. The overdraft was up to £40,000. The shareholders considered a call of £5 per share to avoid liquidation. The call was successful, but liquidation still threatened, particularly if the bank were to withdraw support. Losses had been £4,852 to March 1878, £9,860 to March 1879 and £3,190 to March 1880. The directors offered to resign, but their offer was not accepted. The board considered winding up, working on till the money ran out or raising more funds. Voluntary liquidation was chosen.

At an extraordinary general meeting on 3 July 1880, the shareholders voted to wind up the Yorkshire Engine Co. Hampson and the Company Secretary Harrison were appointed joint liquidators. During the liquidation there were various expressions of interest, including one from Neilson, the locomotive manufacturers, and another from the Agricultural & General Engineering Co. Neither was prepared to pay what the directors considered a fair price of about £60,000. The liquidators ran the company for three and a half years. Turnover gradually increased from £27,342 in the twelve months to June 1881 to £58,469 in the year to June 1883. Profits of £9,419 were made during the liquidation.

In September 1883 a resolution was passed to set up a new Yorkshire Engine Co. with a capital of £60,000, being 2,400 £25 shares. The existing shareholders were offered £10 in cash per old share or a credit of £15 towards the cost of shares in the new Yorkshire Engine Co. Most agreed to subscribe for shares in the new company. Harrison was of the view that the capital was too small, but the shareholders proceeded with their plans. The typical investment in the old company had been fifty £100 shares or £5,000, equivalent to perhaps £250,000 in 2008. If an original investor took shares in the new company in 1883 valued at £15, they would have lost £4,250 on their original investment, equivalent to a loss of about £215,000 in 2008. As a shareholder had pointed out at the 1879 annual meeting, investors had expected to make about 10 per cent on their share capital, when they invested in 1865, this being the return on Sharp Stewart shares at the time. The same investor recognised that no locomotive manufacturing business was now making a return of that order and most, like the Yorkshire Engine Co., were losing money.

Notes

1. *The Fairlie Locomotive Part I* by P.C. Dewhurst, Newcomen Society paper, April 1962.
2. *Locomotive*, 15 December 1909, p.225, states the Bury Port & Gwendraeth locomotive was built in 1873 by the Yorkshire Engine Co.
3. Dewhurst Part I, pp.109–112, and Yorkshire Engine Co. drawing office order book, April and September 1873 and January 1875.
4. *The Fairlie Locomotive* by R.A.S. Abbott, p.43 and 46.
5. Drawings are available in the Sheffield Archives for the following Fairlie patent locomotives: YE170, 175, 190, 219, 446, 834.
6. *Locomotive*, 15 November 1950, p.168
7. *Locomotive*, 14 December 1929, p.384, and *SLS Journal*, January 1953, p.14.
8. *The Nitrate Railways Company Limited* by Donald Binns, p.5; also *Locomotive*, 15 March 1932, p.85.
9. *The Nitrate Railways Company Limited* by Donald Binns, p.7.
10. *Transcaucasian Railway* by R.A.S. Hennessey, pp.19–21.
11. *The Nitrate Railways Company Limited* by Donald Binns, p.51.
12. *Locomotive*, November 1911, pp.249–252.
13. The letter about Fairlie's visit, which was mentioned in correspondence with Dewhurst in 1962 (Dewhurst Part II pages 20 and 21), is not in archives transferred to Sheffield following the closure of the Yorkshire Engine Co.
14. Order number 2283 from 'T. Vancamp' YEC2/2 drawing office order book.
15. Drawing office order book, April 1874, reference 2442.
16. Order book, 8 March 1878, reference 3300.
17. This story comes from an article by David L. Smith on the Wigtownshire Railway in *Locomotive*, 15 August 1943, p.119, and is repeated in his book *Little Railways of South West Scotland* (David & Charles 1969). No original sources are given.
18. *Steam on the RENFE* by L.G. Marshall, p.118.
19. *Beyer Peacock History* by R. Hills and D. Patrick.
20. *Stephenson Locomotive Society Journal*, July/August 1947, p.151.

3

The Hampson Years
1884–1906

Robert Hampson had proved he could run the company profitably during the liquidation. The new board, still with Thomas Vickers as Chairman, appointed Hampson as Manager of the new Yorkshire Engine Co. He was awarded a five-year contract at a salary of £500 a year and a profit-related bonus. Harrison, who had shared the liquidator role with Hampson, retained the post of Company Secretary on a salary of £350 a year. Harrison left his post due to ill-health in December 1885 and did not return when his health recovered. The new board included a mining engineer, a cotton bleacher, a food wholesaler and several 'gentlemen'. At its first meeting in January 1884 the board awarded both Hampson and Harrison a bonus of £150 for their successful conclusion of the liquidation.

Hampson had been with the company for nineteen years when he was finally put in sole charge. He was to run the Yorkshire Engine Co. successfully for another twenty-two years until he handed over the role to a new General Manager in April 1906. Robert Schofield Hampson was born in Dukinfield, Cheshire, in 1838. His father was a proprietor of land and houses. Robert was the youngest of six children and appears to have retained a house in Dukinfield at least until he became Manager of the Yorkshire Engine Co. He and his wife Elizabeth had three daughters – Ada, Esther Gertrude and Minnie. The family lived on Norwood Road, Sheffield. Workmen from the Yorkshire Engine Co. undertook repairs to their house when required. They had two servants – a cook and a general maid.

Hampson's close understanding of the works enabled him to seek and often obtain orders to match the capacity of the plant and the skills of the workforce. Where this was advantageous, he would refuse orders for new locomotives and take in repair work or subcontract machining. To keep the boiler shop busy, he developed a trade in replacement boilers for Yorkshire Engine Co. locomotives and for locomotives made by other manufacturers, including those made in the railway companies' own workshops. He took the company into the production of mining machinery and developed a network of agents in major UK cities. At this time most UK-owned railways in India, South America and elsewhere had UK-based agents as the contact point for purchases from Britain.

During its first six years to 1890 the new Yorkshire Engine Co. had mixed fortunes. In the first year to December 1884 profits of £5,699 were made after depreciation of £2,000 and a 5 per cent dividend was paid. Sales and profits fell for the next two years to a low of £634 in 1886. The dividend of 5 per cent was maintained at a cost of £1,500. Orders and profits then recovered steadily and by 1890 were back at 1884 levels with a 10 per cent dividend paid on profits of £5,888 after £2,000 depreciation. This level of profit was achieved in a period when the Yorkshire Engine Co.'s output of new locomotives was lower than it had ever been in its history.

Only thirty new locomotives were delivered in the first six years of the new Yorkshire Engine Co., an average of five a year. The works was operating at about 10 per cent of its theoretical capacity. Prices for locomotives were low for much of the period and Hampson told the board in June 1886 that he would concentrate on business from local steelworks, including iron and brass castings. He would employ his

Buenos Ayres Great Southern was supplied with five 0-6-0Ts in 1884 (YE378–382); originally numbered 61–65, they were subsequently renumbered 16–20. (LM p.33)

fitters on maintenance work on stationary engines. Hampson together with Sugden, who was in charge of the works, and Ogden, who worked in the office and handled estimates, were all told to get out and seek repairs from local firms. To strengthen the sales effort agents were appointed during 1886–7 in Liverpool, Ireland, Hull, Birmingham and Canada. The agents received between 2.5 per cent and 5 per cent commission on sales. In June 1887 Hunt lost the exclusive London agency he and Edward Sacré had enjoyed for over twenty years; he was told he would still receive a 5 commission on any orders he placed with the Yorkshire Engine Co. This was reduced in 1888 to 2.5 per cent on all business except locomotives where the commission was to be only 1 per cent.

The American continent continued to be an important market up to 1891. The first locomotive deliveries in 1884 were to an old customer, the Buenos Aires Great Southern. The railway, which had bought its first six 2-4-0Ts in 1871–2 from the Yorkshire Engine Co. and ten 4-4-0Ts in 1874–5, acquired five 0-6-0Ts (YE378–382). It also purchased a total of four replacement boilers in the period up to 1890 as well as a quantity of spares. Other South American customers to return included the Nitrate Railways. A 0-4-0ST (YE427) was acquired via their agents Ward J. Lockett in 1888 and two more Fairlie 0-6-6-0s in 1890 (YE442–3) and a boiler. The Mexican Southern Railway, a new 280-mile line running from Puebla to Oaxaca, ordered two 3ft-gauge 0-6-0Ts to be named *Mariscal* and *Dublan* in 1889 (YE435–6). A year later in 1891 the Anglo Chilean Nitrate & Railway Co. bought two 3ft 6in-gauge 0-6-6-0 Fairlies (YE446–447). This company operated a 184-mile line connecting two large nitrate plants, Maria Elena and Pedro de Valdivia, with the port of Tocopilla. The line reached a height of 4,500ft. The two Fairlies were built to the Yorkshire Engine Co.'s design and were the only Fairlies used on the line. They were withdrawn about 1929.

During Hampson's time with the Yorkshire Engine Co. and particularly his last fifteen years from 1891 to 1906, overseas sales remained important, but less significant as UK business developed. The South Indian Railway bought four metre-gauge 0-4-4Ts for £1,380 each in 1885 (YE399–402). The Sindi, Punjab & Delhi Railway ordered five boilers in 1885. The Bombay, Baroda & Central India acquired two 0-4-2s for His Highness the Gaekwar's State Railway in 1891 (YE463–4) and three very similar 0-4-2s were supplied to the Ankleshwar Pardi Railway in 1896 (YE528–530). The Indian State Railways also ordered fourteen boilers and the Southern Mahratta twelve boilers in 1904–5. The Great Indian Peninsular railway was a major customer for spares.

The 3ft-gauge Mexican Southern acquired two 0-6-0Ts (YE435–6) from the Yorkshire Engine Co. and named them Mariscal and Dublan. (LM p.32)

YE447 was one of two Fairlies built for the 3ft 6in-gauge Anglo Chilean Nitrate & Railway Co. in 1891. (Derek Penney Collection)

Four metre-gauge 0-4-4Ts were delivered to the South Indian Railway in 1881; initially numbered 121–124 they were renumbered D1-4 (YE401). (LM p.29)

H.H. Gaekwar's State Railway, a section of the Bombay Baroda & Central India 2ft 6in-gauge line, bought two (YE463–4) 0-4-2s in 1891; note the warning bell on the tender for the guard to ring in the event of a problem. (LM p.20)

Four 0-4-2s, nos 9–11, went to the Ankleshwar Pardi Railway in 1896 (YE528). (LM p.18)

In Australia the Queensland Government Railway bought ten 4-6-0s with eight-wheeled tenders in 1896–7 (YE531–540). This was the largest single order in the period. The locomotives were sold for £1,760 each and the Yorkshire Engine Co. made a loss of £1,287 on the contract. No.532 (Queensland Railways No.290) survives awaiting the removal of asbestos cladding in a shed at the Ipswich Railway Workshops in Queensland. Elsewhere in Australia Southern Coal acquired two 0-6-0STs (YE428–9) in 1888. Numbered 1 and 2, No.1 survived on colliery work in and around Queensland till 1964 and No.2 till 1968, when they were scrapped.[1]

In 1904–5 four locomotives were supplied to the Junin Railway. Like the other railways serving the nitrate mines, this 2ft 6in-gauge line had to cope with a steep ascent from the coastal plain. The line climbed 1,680ft in thirty-two miles with gradients of 1:35 and curves of 230ft radius. The Yorkshire Engine Co. first supplied two 0-6-2STs in 1904 (YE791–2) and then in the following year two modified Fairlie 0-6-6-0s (YE834–5) named *San Antonio* and *Compania*. The locomotives had two entirely separate boilers on a single deep girder frame, which made maintaining water levels easier. The engines weighed 52 tons 2cwt with 1,500 gallons of water and 2 tons of coal. To avoid some of the problems encountered by earlier Fairlies, the arrangement of the steam pipes was improved and simplified. The pipes were lagged with asbestos to reduce condensation and only one ball joint was required immediately above the centre of the bogie, so that movement was minimised. The Yorkshire Engine Co. board hoped these improvements would lead to more orders for Fairlies, but this was

Ten 3ft 6in-gauge 4-6-0s were supplied by the Yorkshire Engine Co. to the Queensland Government Railway in 1896–7 (YE538). (LM p.12)

One of the Queensland Government Railway 4-6-0s, photographed in October 2004, still survives at the Ipswich Railway workshops in 2008 (YE532). (Ed Slee)

The Yorkshire Engine Co. supplied the first two 0-6-0STs to Southern Coal of New South Wales, Australia in 1888 (YE428–9). (LM p.30)

Recuerdo was one of two 0-6-2STs bought by the Junin Railway, a 2ft 6in-gauge line in Chile, in 1904 (YE792). (LM p.25)

The Junin Railway was one of the last lines in the nitrate fields to try Fairlie locomotives; the two 0-6-6-0s bought from the Yorkshire Engine Co. in 1905 were called San Antonio (YE834) and Compania and were to be the Yorkshire Engine Co.'s last Fairlies. (Derek Penney Collection)

not to be.² Meyer-type articulated locomotives were slowly to replace Fairlies on the railways in the nitrate mining area.

An important customer during the last two decades of the nineteenth century was the War Office. Construction of the Chattendon & Upnor Railway began in 1873. The railway consisted of about four miles of track linking various Naval and military depots and barracks. Pontoon Hard and Upnor depots, both on the River Medway opposite Chatham docks, were linked to Chattenden depot and barracks and Lodge Hill enclosure. The 8th Railway Co. of the Royal Engineers managed the line till 1905 and used it for training and the transport of men and stores. Laid to 2ft 6in gauge, the Yorkshire Engine Co. supplied two 0-4-2Ts named *Carbon* and *Sulphur* in 1885 (YE404–405). A 0-4-4T was supplied in 1891 (YE462) somewhat perversely named *Lancashire*. Two more locomotives were supplied to what was now called the Lodge Hill and Upnor Railway in 1902 and 1904. *Lord Kitchener* was a 0-6-2T (YE711) and *Pioneer* a 2-6-2 pannier tank (YE757). *Lord Kitchener* saw service in Egypt and *Pioneer* subsequently had a spell at the Longmoor Military Railway and then on the St Austell & Pentewan Railway, before moving to the War Department at Sunbury. *Pioneer* was of unusual design with bar and plate frames, Walschaerts valve gear and equipment for oil firing.³ The War Office also bought two metre-gauge 0-6-0Ts in 1898, one of which later went to the Longitudinal Railway in Chile (YE 554–5), another line in the nitrate area of Chile, and a four-wheeled electric locomotive in 1890 (YE 468).

The War Office bought more than locomotives during the period. In 1887 two boilers were built for Cliff End Fort and Fort Ricasoli in Malta. From 1889 the Yorkshire Engine Co. had useful business

Carbon (YE404) was one of two 2ft 6in-gauge 0-4-2Ts supplied to the War Office for the Chattenden & Upnor Railway in 1885. (LM p.36)

The Yorkshire Engine Co. supplied Lancashire (YE462), an 0-4-4T, to the War Office for the Chattenden & Upnor in 1891. (LM p.35)

Lord Kitchener (YE711), an 0-6-2T, was the fourth locomotive supplied by the Yorkshire Engine Co. to the Chattenden & Upnor. (LM p.23)

building twenty ammunition lifts. Both right-hand and left-hand lifts were built for 38-ton guns. The lifts had to be able to raise ammunition 30ft. The Secretary of State for War remained a major customer till Hampson retired in 1906.

The largest single customer for locomotive business during the Hampson era was the Great Central Railway (GCR), the renamed Manchester Sheffield and Lincolnshire Railway. Although the Hull & Barnsley bought twenty-one locomotives and the GCR only fifteen during the period ending in 1906, the GCR was still the Yorkshire Engine Co.'s single most important customer due to the quantity of locomotive overhauls and boilers supplied. Substantial orders for boilers and other repairs also came from the London, Brighton & South Coast Railway (LBSCR), the Midland and the Great Western railways. In late 1898 the board asked for a list of future orders. The bulk of the £65,000 orders were from sixteen customers and 30 per cent of the value of those orders came from the GCR:

Customer	Value £
Great Central Railway	19,500
Hull and Barnsley	8,000
Secretary of State for War	6,530
Cammell Church & Co	5,200
Thomas Firth & Sons	3,660
Vickers Sons & Maxim	3,600
London, Brighton & South Coast Railway	3,000
Sharp Stewart & Co	2,700
Woodhouse & Rixon	1,600
Moira Colliery	1,500
Tayler Brothers & Co	1,450

A total of fifteen Great Central 0-6-0s with six-wheeled tenders were made by the Yorkshire Engine Co. between 1904 and 1906; the Class 9J was Robinson's first goods locomotive nicknamed the Pompom and No. 1119 was the last one built by the Yorkshire Engine Co. in 1906 (YE858). (LM p.6)

Steel Peech & Tozer	875
Midland Railway	860
Neath & Brecon Railway	1,600
Metropolitan Railway	580
Bolton Iron & Steel	470
Total	61,125

In spite of his links with the Yorkshire Engine Co., Charles Sacré had never provided much business to the company when he was in charge of the MSLR's locomotive department. The pattern changed under Harry Pollitt, who replaced Sacré's successor Thomas Parker in 1893, and John Robinson, who succeeded Pollitt in 1900. Robinson's first goods locomotive was a 0-6-0, a development from Pollitt's 0-6-0s with a larger firebox and an increased cylinder size. Known as GCR Class 9J (LNER J11), 174 locomotives were built at both the GCR's own works at Gorton and by outside manufacturers. The Yorkshire Engine Co. built a total of fifteen (YE765–769, 820–824 and 854–858) between 1904 and 1906. The first five were built for £2,850, the price charged by Beyer Peacock. The price left no margin for general expenses and the subsequent order was also tightly priced. The final five, built by the Yorkshire Engine Co. in 1906, were constructed with a boiler pressure of 200psi, higher than the normal pressure for the class, and for a better price of £3,300 per locomotive. The psi on these five Yorkshire Engine Co. locomotives was subsequently reduced to the normal 180psi for the class. Boiler pressure for all the class was then reduced to 160psi as an economy measure. The engines were known as 'Pom-Poms' because of the similarity of their exhaust note to a quick-firing gun called the 'Pom-Pom'.

More important for the Yorkshire Engine Co. than the new locomotive orders was a huge locomotive refurbishment programme for the GCR. The first orders were placed in November 1897 by Harry Pollitt. A total of twelve Sacré 0-6-0s and tenders were booked in for refurbishment. A second order for the overhaul of another fifteen 0-6-0s was placed in April 1899. When Pollitt reported to the GCR Board in August 1899, he noted that 153 out of a total fleet of 902 engines were under repair, of which thirteen were then with the Yorkshire Engine Co. Gorton Works did not have the capacity to undertake all the repairs.[4]

In spite of Pollitt's efforts, much of the GCR's locomotive stock was still in poor repair when J.G. Robinson took over. Another ten GCR locomotives came to Meadowhall in 1900 for overhaul, together with orders for boilers. Robinson had concluded that around 100 boilers and fireboxes were needed and the Yorkshire Engine Co. offered the most competitive price at £760 per boiler. Nine firms had tendered and the Yorkshire Engine Co. was the cheapest by £20. Stephensons, Vulcan and Dubs had all quoted

Hull & Barnsley Railway purchased a total of fifteen 0-6-0 goods locomotives with six-wheel tenders from the Yorkshire Engine Co. between 1897 and 1900; this illustration shows the penultimate locomotive No.95 (YE608) ready to leave Meadowhall. (LM p.10)

£780. Sharp Stewart was the most expensive at £850.[5] Six boilers had been supplied to the GCR in 1899; twenty were delivered in 1901 and another twenty later the same year. Penalties of £20 per month could be imposed if the boilers were delivered late. More orders followed in 1902. It may well have been the quality of the Yorkshire Engine Co.'s work on locomotive overhauls which encouraged the GCR to give the Yorkshire Engine Co. the orders for new locomotives in 1904–6.

Two other significant UK railways placed their first orders for new locomotives with the Yorkshire Engine Co. in the Hampson era. Both continued to be customers in subsequent years. The larger of the two was the Hull & Barnsley, where Matthew Stirling was Locomotive Superintendent. Matthew had trained under his father Patrick at the GNR and joined the Hull & Barnsley on its formation in 1885. Like his father he tended to favour domeless boilers and spartan cabs. Matthew's first design was a 0-6-0, a key locomotive type for a railway reliant on the mineral trade. A total of fifty-five Hull & Barnsley Class Bs (LNER Class J23) was built between 1889 and 1908 by three manufacturers – Kitson, the Vulcan Foundry and the Yorkshire Engine Co. The Yorkshire Engine Co.'s first order for six locomotives was delivered in 1897 and another batch of three followed in 1898 and a final six in 1900 (YE547–552, 560–562 and 604–609). The locomotives operated at a boiler pressure of 170psi and weighed 78 tons 15cwt. The LNER fitted new boilers to many of the class in the 1920s. They were withdrawn between 1930 and 1938.

Hampson made sure he kept in regular contact with Matthew Stirling. The Hull & Barnsley placed a further order with the Yorkshire Engine Co. for six 0-6-0Ts to be delivered in 1901–2. Based on an earlier class of shunting locomotives, a total of sixteen Class G2s (LNER Class J80) were built. This time the Yorkshire Engine Co. built the first batch of six (YE655–660). Again with boiler pressure of 170psi and a weight of 46 tons 17cwt, the locomotives were initially used on the Wath and Braithwell branches. Sadly for the Yorkshire Engine Co. the company did not receive the follow-up order for another ten of the same locomotives in 1908. Kitson obtained the business.[6]

A further significant railway to place its first Yorkshire Engine Co. order in 1901 was the Metropolitan. It is difficult today to imagine the Metropolitan Railway as a freight carrier, but in 1900 freight traffic was growing on the line which extended out through Aylesbury to Verney Junction in Buckinghamshire. To handle the freight traffic, much of which came from the GCR, T.F. Clark, Chief Mechanical Engineer, ordered four 0-6-2Ts from the Yorkshire Engine Co. (YE624–627). These were called Class F and were a development of Clark's Class E 0-4-4s, which were used for passenger traffic. Equipped with condensing arrangements for underground working, the locomotives weighed 58 tons in working order and were 35ft 3in in length over the buffers. They proved capable of handling the Metropolitan's heaviest goods trains.[7]

The industrial locomotive business continued to provide some stability at Meadowhall. Although requiring prior board approval, 0-4-0STs were regularly built for stock. Both 12in and 14in cylinder sizes

The first batch of six 0-6-0T s was supplied by the Yorkshire Engine Co. to the Hull & Barnsley in 1901–2 (YE660). (LM p.15)

were now used. Eventually in December 1891 the board agreed four stock tank engines should always be under construction or in hand. In the twenty-two years between 1884 and 1906 thirty-two 0-4-0STs were sold to industry, including collieries, steelworks and engineering firms, and one 0-6-0ST (YE799) to the Hepworth Iron Co. Colliery customers for 0-4-0STs included Wharncliffe Silkstone, Wharncliffe Woodmoor, Chatterley Whitfield, Hoyland Silkstone, Nunnery and Moira Collieries. Charles Cammell purchased five locomotives.

With a mining engineer on the board, an existing customer base in the mining industry and the requisite engineering skills, it made sense for the Yorkshire Engine Co. to introduce new products for this market. The first recorded order for a pair of haulage engines was in 1888 to the Rothervale Colliery. The first two coal-cutting machines are recorded as being ordered by Wharncliffe Silkstone in 1889. However this order requests a machine to the design supplied to the Lidgett Colliery. George Blake Walker, who was agent for the Lidgett Colliery, was also a director of Yorkshire Engine. It seems plausible that, when considering the introduction of their coal cutter, the Yorkshire Engine Co. should have asked Lidgett to try the machine first before offering it to other customers. Lidgett Colliery already had a good working relationship with the Yorkshire Engine Co. It had repaired Lidgett's sole steam locomotive *Success* on several occasions both on site and at Meadowhall. It had hired out a locomotive to Lidgett when its own locomotive was out of action. To meet such needs the Yorkshire Engine Co. board had bought a second-hand locomotive for hiring out in March 1885.[8]

To develop the market for mining products, the board agreed to build some coal cutters for stock. It also appointed an agent in June 1889 to cover the northern coal fields. Sales of coal cutters grew and in June 1890 three more machines were built for stock. Emerson Bainbridge, who had taken the chair following the death of Thomas Vickers, suggested a sales leaflet should be prepared to show the benefits of the Yorkshire Engine Co.'s mining products and letters were sent to all colliery managers. By October of the following year the board was considering building haulage engines as well as coal cutters for stock. The Yorkshire Engine Co. would provide on-site help to collieries to explain how to get the best from their coal cutters. As the business developed a second agent was appointed in 1897. Both received 5 per cent on sales. In 1894 Nunnery Colliery was allowed a machine to try for three months at a cost of £50 plus making good any damage. Two years later in 1896 the company was considering introducing other designs offered by independent engineers, but concluded it was better to update their own machines with compressed air or electricity. The board eventually agreed to try a new coal cutter designed by a Mr Haggis in 1905. The board was still at this time debating whether they should drive their own cutter by electricity. A total of sixty-four coal cutters of various types were made between 1889 and Hampson's retirement in 1906. Sales of coal cutters continued till the First World War. Haulage engine sales were developed thereafter and continued till the 1940s.

Metropolitan Railway's three 0-6-2Ts were supplied in 1901; No.93 was the last of the batch (YE627). (LM p.13)

A 0-6-0ST (YE799) was supplied to Hepworth Iron in 1905 and was still in action at Penistone some fifty-five years later in April 1960. (Alec Swain – Transport Treasury)

Amongst the other more unusual products supplied by the Yorkshire Engine Co. were rack rails. Charles Cammell, which continued to be one of Yorkshire Engine Co.'s best customers, rolled the rails and cut them to size, typically 12ft or 15ft lengths. The Yorkshire Engine Co.'s job was to cut the teeth in the rails and assemble the track work. The first customer was the Snowdon Mountain Railway in 1895, for which firm 7,893m of rack rail were 'toothed' and crossings constructed. 2,370m of rail were produced for the Mount Morgan Railway in Australia in 1897 and orders were received for the Nilghri rack railway in India in December 1898 and for Japan in May 1905.[9] The rails were clamped to a machine bed plate and

The Yorkshire Engine Co. produced over eighty coal cutting machines between 1890 and 1914. This machine is powered by a two-cylinder compressed air engine. The powered rope winch on the far left would drag the machine along the coal face. (Sheffield Archives)

cut from solid by a rotary toothed drum. The machine was located in a corner of the machine shop next to the drawing office, where the junior draughtsman had his desk. He was glad that the machine was used somewhat infrequently.[10]

The management structure of the Yorkshire Engine Co. was strengthened as the company developed under Hampson's guidance. H.C. Jenkinson from nearby Wincobank was appointed Secretary in July 1888 at a salary of £180 per year. Hampson had fulfilled the secretarial duties since the departure of the last Secretary in 1886. Ogden provided a report to the board on sales each month; in addition reports were tabled by Hampson and the Secretary. In April 1889 Hampson was given a new five-year contract. He asked to be appointed Managing Director. His request was refused, but his salary increased to £600 a year with a discretionary bonus. In January 1890 the pay of the new Secretary, Jenkinson, was increased to £250 and Sugden appointed Assistant Manager on £300 a year plus a bonus of 1 per cent of profits. Hampson asked for the same profit share deal, but was refused. Nonetheless, the board changed their mind the following month and put his salary up to £700 per year and gave him the bonus plan he wanted.

In 1896 Hampson received the appointment he craved and was appointed Managing Director on an unchanged salary. He had been with the company thirty years. His pay was eventually reviewed in May 1898, when he received an increase to £750 a year plus a tripled profit share to 3 per cent of profits. The Secretary's bonus was increased to 2 per cent of profits. In July 1901 the company received a letter from Harry Pollitt asking if he could be appointed the Yorkshire Engine Co.'s agent in Australia. When Pollitt retired from the Locomotive Engineer post at the Great Central, he and his wife had moved to Australia. The board agreed to Pollitt's appointment and sent him £200 to help him get started. Pollitt only held the post for two years till July 1903, when he had to return to United Kingdom due to ill health.

The board valued their top team of Hampson, Sugden and Jenkinson. In January 1904 Hampson's pay went up to £1,000 per year and his two senior colleagues to £350. However, the board seems to have doubted the ability of Sugden or Jenkinson to succeed Hampson. In September 1904, when Pollitt's health had recovered and he approached the Yorkshire Engine Co. for a job, the board made him assistant to Hampson on £500 a year. Pollitt was given a six-year agreement terminable at six months' notice by either party – the appointment was not a success. Pollitt was expected to visit potential customers and solicit orders. He failed to bring in new customers and in January 1906, as the Yorkshire Engine Co. plant was now fully occupied in spite of Pollitt's lack of success, he was asked to move into the works to assist Hampson. He was given a season ticket for travel to and from London and told to report on the state of the works and suggest improvements. The Chairman liked his ideas but expressed some disappointment that the proposals were not costed and no assessment had been made of the potential savings from the suggested improvements. If the board had considered Pollitt as a potential successor to Hampson, they were now having serious doubts.

Between 1888 and 1893 the Yorkshire Engine Co. produced a total of four cranes for Park Gate Iron and Steel and Charles Cammell; this 15-ton machine (YE511) was built for Parkgate in June 1893. (Sheffield Archives)

With the exception of 1892, when a loss of £871 was incurred, the Yorkshire Engine Co. had a period of unrivalled prosperity from 1890 to 1905 under the leadership of Hampson and his Chairman, Emerson Bainbridge. In 1899 profits exceeded £12,000 for the first time and the company was able to pay a dividend of 25 per cent on its shares, which had been changing hands at or below £25 in 1898 and were worth over £50 by March 1900. An approach was made to acquire the business by the MSLR in 1893 and by another firm in 1899. Both came to nothing. The board reorganised the share structure to give shareholders a preference share paying 5 per cent, so that excessively high dividends were not paid on the ordinary shares. One shareholder expressed concern that this would leave little in reserve if difficult times returned.

At a board meeting on 4 April 1906, the directors agreed it was time to find a new General Manager. Hampson had reached the age of sixty-eight and concurred. It was agreed Hampson would receive his full salary of £1,000 per year to April 1907 and £500 a year for the next two years. Profits had been falling for the last two years and substantial sums spent on improvements to the works. The board believed some lucrative sources of business were coming to an end and decided they needed to appoint a new manager with wide experience of the engineering trade. Interviews were held in London and Mr Watson Foggo was selected. He was aged forty-three; he had held a number of posts in collieries and general engineering works, but had no railway locomotive experience. He had most recently been employed by Clayton Shuttleworth of Lincoln, best known at the time as manufacturers of steam traction engines and threshing machines. He was offered a five-year contract at £800 a year and a commission of 5 per cent of net profits. Pollitt, having realised that he was not to get the Managing Director post, had tendered his resignation in March 1906.

Notes

1. *Industrial Steam Locomotives Illawarra District New South Wales* from the Australian Railway Historical Society, December 1983.
2. R.A.S. Abbott, p.48; *Locomotive Magazine*, 15 January 1907, pp.7–8.
3. *Lodge Hill & Upnor Railway*, D. Yeatman IRR, December 1966, pp.277–292.
4. *Locomotives of the Great Central Railway* by E.M. Johnson, Volume 1, p.2.
5. *Locomotives of the Great Central Railway*, Volume 1, p.4.
6. *Locomotive Magazine* 1902, p.113.
7. *Locomotive Magazine*, May 1901, and www.railwayarchive.org.uk, T.F. Clark and Charles Jones locomotives.
8. Information on the Lidgett Colliery was drawn from *Lidgett Colliery* by Trevor J. Lodge IRR, No.54, pp.237–252.
9. IRR February 1971, p.21, Snowdon Rack Railway; board minutes and drawing office order book.
10. *SLS Journal*, March 1976, C.B. Harley, p.73.

4

New Management and New Ventures 1906–1919

Watson Foggo took over from Hampson in June 1906 and prospects for the Yorkshire Engine Co. looked good. Orders had risen from £61,816 in 1904 to £104,807 in 1905 and were to reach £138,811 in 1907. Foggo immediately put in a request for new plant and by September the board had agreed improvements to the boiler shop and copper smiths. Shares were changing hands at £19 and the preference shares at par. However, profits for the year to December 1906 were a modest £3,634 and a 5 per cent dividend was the maximum the company could afford, as expansion had lead to a cash shortage and a rising overdraft.

At the annual meeting in March 1907 the Chairman, Emerson Bainbridge, said 'a new and successful epoch in the history of the company' is opening up. He mentioned the many improvements to the works and listed a number of significant contracts:

Hull & Barnsley Railway 15 engines and tenders (YE 899–908 and 942–946)
London, Brighton & South Coast Railway 10 locomotives for repair plus 15 boilers
Great Indian Peninsular Railway 13 locomotive boilers
Nitrate Railways 2 locomotives (YE 940–941) plus 2 Fairlie boilers
South Eastern & Chatham Railway – several unspecified contracts

The Chairman advised the shareholders that the company had entered into the business of making car chassis 'on an absolutely safe basis' with a London-based syndicate called 'Motor House' or 'Grande Maison d'Automobile'. First discussions on the manufacture of motor cars must have taken place as soon as Foggo took over, for an order for ten chassis is recorded in the drawing office order book for July 1906. In January 1907 Foggo told the board an agreement had been received that morning from Motor House regarding the manufacture of fifty additional motor chassis. The Chairman immediately asked for the value of purchases and the manufacturing costs to be thoroughly investigated. A month later Foggo reported that it would cost £10,000 to alter the works to make cars. Hampson disagreed with this expenditure, but two directors were authorised to sign the contract with Motor House.

The first complete car was available for the shareholders to see and try following the annual meeting in March 1907. The Chairman told the meeting the agreement to make car chassis was excellent 'unless (Mr Foggo) has made a very serious mistake in his estimate of the cost of manufacture of these cars'. The extra expenditure required the overdraft to be increased. Cash became even tighter and Foggo had to turn down new locomotive orders. No stock tank locomotives were to be made in order to conserve working capital.

Car manufacture did not proceed smoothly. The first ten chassis had to be modified and the Yorkshire Engine Co. picked up the cost. Purchasers often wanted special modifications and repairs had to be undertaken if faults developed. In August 1907 a car for a Mr Lane had to have a new gear box and carburettor and an order was received for an experimental chassis for a six-cylinder car.[1] Repairs were undertaken on Mr Simpson's racing car in October. The directors were becoming concerned as to whether Motor House had the right to call their car Daimler Mercedes (British) and asked for an indemnity.

Matthew Stirling ordered an initial ten 0-8-0s from Yorkshire Engine for the Hull & Barnsley's heavy coal traffic in 1906 to avoid using double-headed 0-6-0s. No. 117 (YE899) was the first engine produced; a further five were supplied in 1907. (LM p.2)

The Yorkshire Engine Co. built two 118-ton Meyer-type 0-6-6-0s (YE940–941) for the Nitrate Railways in 1906; they were scrapped in the early 1930s. (LM p.1)

A complete Yorkshire Engine Co. car out on the road; this may be the test car shown to shareholders at the annual meeting in March 1907. (Sheffield Archives)

The car was identical to the 30hp Mercedes Daimler and it would appear that royalties for the use of the name were paid on the initial vehicles, but the syndicate behind the venture subsequently refused to make further payments.[2] Orders for parts for the fifty chassis were deferred due to a shortage of cash.

The financial position was becoming more difficult. The board resolved to make additional calls on the shareholders and debentures were issued to the bank, now part of the Williams Deacons group, at 5 per cent interest. Motor House was unwilling to increase the contract price per chassis. The board decided to see if they could get the chassis made by a third party. Sheffield Simplex quoted £300 per chassis, a price the Yorkshire Engine Co. could not contemplate. Hampson went to see Vickers, Son & Maxim, an established major Yorkshire Engine Co. customer, who rejected the chassis work without quoting.

As a result of the general disruption to the works from the construction of cars and the substantial increase in orders, locomotive business was falling behind schedule. The Hull & Barnsley had gone elsewhere for new work and refused to make a £3,000 payment due on their engines as a result of late delivery. The South East & Chatham imposed penalties for late delivery and the Crown Agents also threatened penalties for late delivery of boilers for the Great Indian Peninsular Railway. The board decided urgent action was needed and asked the auditors to take charge of the offices and finances and to introduce a new costing system.

Emerson Bainbridge concluded in October 1907 that he could not continue as Chairman and handed over to George Blake Walker, a mining engineer who had been on the board for some years. A works committee was set up to meet every Wednesday to review work in progress with Foggo. Hampson was asked to spend a day a week in the works, for experienced management was becoming very thin. Edward Sugden, who had been with the firm for forty years and was Assistant Manager under Hampson, had died in March 1907; in December the Works Manager had left. One of the foremen, Haynes, was found to be inadequate and uninterested in the motor chassis work. Relations with Motor House were deteriorating and litigation was threatened. The accounts for the year to December 1907 showed a loss of £11,695.

The annual shareholders' meeting to review the results for 1907 took place earlier than usual in February 1908. Blake Walker, now Chairman, stated: 'It is a bad report, so bad you must feel bewildered to understand how things can have so completely changed since the last meeting of shareholders… When the auditor told the directors in July we had lost £10,000 we could hardly believe it.' The Chairman then told the shareholders that another £4,000 of disputed liabilities had to be added to the near £12,000 loss shown in the accounts. Some £8,000 of unauthorised expenditure had been incurred in the works. £570 per engine or a total of £5,700 had been lost on the ten Hull & Barnsley engines already delivered and £200 had been lost on each of the thirteen boilers for the Great Indian Peninsular Railway. Foggo had to take most of the blame, although some orders had been taken in Hampson's time. Foggo had been unwilling to take advice from Hampson and the death of Sugden exacerbated the problems.

The shareholders were critical of the board for relying on written references for Foggo and not speaking to his former employers. Foggo tried to defend himself by saying the Yorkshire Engine Co. had never made money on new locomotives and that the works was in a poor state so production costs were higher than they would have been in a modern plant. Foggo had experienced difficulty with the railway inspectors sent to check products before delivery and complained that the inspectors did not like the change of management. Foggo's lack of locomotive experience can not have helped his relationships with the railway companies. Not surprisingly the shareholders refused to ratify Foggo's appointment as Managing Director.

Following the annual meeting, Blake Walker stepped down as Chairman and was replaced by Frederick Jones. Jones had been educated at Repton and Trinity College, Cambridge. He played a leading role in the commercial and industrial life of South Yorkshire and was head of the Rothervale Collieries, an important Yorkshire Engine Co. customer. When becoming a director, he had bought his shares at par, not realising the poor state of the business. Jones and Moss, who was also a member of the Yorkshire Engine Co. board, were asked to undertake a review of the company's business and report back to shareholders in four months. The board decided that Foggo should 'retire' on 31 May 1908. The board could not afford

Nine complete cars are lined up in the Meadowhall works. These are probably nine of the ten chassis completed under the first order during the summer of 1907. (Derek Penney Collection)

to pay him off outright and agreed to give him £200 per year for four years. Jones and Moss would act as Joint Managing Directors. A Mr J.D.R. Phillips had been appointed General Manager on 1 June at a salary of £450 a year. The board admitted that Phillips was not necessarily of the calibre they would have liked. However, he had locomotive experience, which accounted for half the revenue, and he was willing to join a business in difficulty at a modest salary.

Jones and Moss reported to the shareholders in June 1908. They stated the damage to the company's reputation was as serious as the damage to its finances. Work had been accepted without regard to cost or capacity. Unprofitable contracts had attracted overtime to avoid or reduce late delivery penalties, although a successful negotiation had brought down the penalty payment to the Hull & Barnsley from £3,340 to £1,500. Very little new locomotive business had come in and, if they were to get any, it would have to be at a very low price till Yorkshire Engine Co.'s reputation was restored. The motor losses were increasing. £8,000 had been spent on parts and there was a commitment to spend another £6,000. The Chairman emphasised that the shareholders should not reveal to others what they had learnt that day, if Yorkshire Engine Co. was to continue in business.

By the time the shareholders met again in March 1909 to review the results to December 1908, some progress had been made. Although turnover had more than halved from £127,297 in 1907 to only £55,556 in 1908, losses had also reduced from £11,695 to £4,664. By the end of 1909, sales had fallen again to £41,371, but losses had been further reduced to £958. There was now some prospect of recovery, although the reduction in turnover meant lay-offs for some of the workforce, short-time working and the end of the night shift. Hampson had been keen to stay on after his consultancy contract ran out in April 1909, but the board decided they could not justify the cost of his continuing services. Shareholders were asked to subscribe another £2 per share to keep the company afloat.

The venture into the motor business continued to cause problems. By March 1909 the contract with Motor House had been cancelled at a cost to the Yorkshire Engine Co. of £2,883, plus a payment for repairs of £1,383. Eighteen chassis had been completed. However, the Yorkshire Engine Co. still had a large stock of parts, which had cost £12,951 but had very little immediate value, as the motor trade was in recession. Attempts were made during 1910 to complete and sell chassis to shareholders, through agents in Holland and on commission via Motor House. All work ceased in the motor department in August

1910. Lists of parts were circulated to motor agents, but few orders arose. Motor House were willing to buy more complete cars and chassis, but their terms were unacceptable to the Yorkshire Engine Co. Motor House had difficulty paying for cars already delivered and in May 1911 a receiver and manager was appointed. The business went into liquidation the following month, leaving the Yorkshire Engine Co. with stocks of chassis and spares which had cost about £16,000. The motor department losses, which still amounted to about £15,000 three years later, were eventually written off following the annual meeting in March 1914. Another experiment, which had nearly brought the Yorkshire Engine Co. down, was at last drawn to a close after eight years. The 'motor department' continued to be so called even when it was subsequently used to build haulage engines for the mines.

From Hampson's retirement as Managing Director in 1906 to the end of the First World War in 1918, the Yorkshire Engine Co. sold seventy-six locomotives. Fifty of these locomotives were supplied to two railway companies, the Hull & Barnsley, which purchased twenty locomotives, and the North British, which purchased thirty. The Metropolitan came back with an order for two locomotives, which was subsequently increased to four. The Nitrate Railways also returned with an order for two unusual locomotives. The bulk of the remaining orders were for standard 0-4-0 and 0-6-0STs for local collieries.

The Yorkshire Engine Co. appear to have been using the adjacent Great Central line for testing locomotives without the permission of the railway; the matter was formally raised on 20 May 1908 in a letter to the Yorkshire Engine Co. board from Sam Fay, General Manager of the Great Central. (Sheffield Archives 1994/8)

Hampson had built up a good relationship with Matthew Stirling of the Hull & Barnsley, which had acquired twenty-one locomotives from the Yorkshire Engine Co. by the time Hampson left the Managing Director role. Stirling's next order for ten 0-8-0s with six-wheeled tenders had been received by the time Foggo took over and a follow-up order for another five followed shortly after (YE 899–908 and 942–946). As the coal trade to Hull's Alexandra Dock increased, Stirling had initially used double-headed 0-6-0s, but this was an unsatisfactory solution. The 0-8-0s were more than a stretched version of the 0-6-0s. The boiler pressure was increased to 200psi and the grate area and cylinders also increased in size. The 0-8-0s were withdrawn in the early years of the Depression from 1929–1931, with some of the boilers being used in former North Eastern Railway 0-8-0s. The initial ten were priced at £3,560, which left the Yorkshire Engine Co. with a loss of £570 per locomotive, but the final five were sold at £4,260 and should have given the Yorkshire Engine Co. a profit.[3] *Locomotive Magazine* described the 0-8-0s as fine engines.

Although the Yorkshire Engine Co. lost out on an order in 1907, the Hull & Barnsley returned to them with an order for five 0-6-0s in April 1913 (YE 1182–1186). Stirling met Moss and a new General Manager, K.W. Willans, who had replaced Phillips, to discuss delivery dates. The Hull & Barnsley failed to provide drawings immediately, which caused some delay. Delivered in 1914, these locomotives were larger and heavier than the 0-6-0s built by the Yorkshire Engine Co. in 1897 and were the last class of 0-6-0s built for the Hull & Barnsley before it was absorbed into the LNER. A total of twenty were built in five batches. The first ten were built by Kitson in 1911–2 and fitted with superheaters. The five Yorkshire Engine Co. engines were slightly heavier than the first ten by Kitson, weighing 51 tons 3cwt, and used saturated steam. The working pressure was 170psi. The final five were built by Kitson. Designed for mineral and fast freight traffic, they were sometimes used double headed. Withdrawals started in 1934.

The order from the North British Railway for thirty 4-4-2Ts was first discussed by the Yorkshire Engine Co. board in February 1911 (YE 1066–1095). The board debated sharing the order with Kitson, but decided to keep the whole order in house, if sufficient funding could be organised. By March the Yorkshire Engine Co. realised it could not find the £40,000 working capital needed before any payment would be made. The Yorkshire Engine Co. Chairman, Frederick Jones, met the North British Chairman and agreed that the first eight engines would be paid for the month after delivery. It was also agreed no penalties would be imposed if locomotives were delivered a few weeks late. In addition the North British agreed to make advance payments for engines nearing completion, if finance caused a problem. With these terms agreed, the bank was then prepared to increase the overdraft to £40,000, subject to a total of £30,000 of debentures and a personal guarantee of £5,000 from the directors.

The North British contract provided two years work for the locomotive department. However, the directors continued to remain concerned that cost estimates might not be accurate. In September 1911 Phillips was asked to confirm he had priced every item of material and labour costs. The Chairman wanted everyone in the works to know what the estimates were, so that there would be no nasty surprises at the end. In January 1912 the Chairman arranged for his twenty-nine-year-old younger son, Charles Frederick Ward Jones, to join the firm to keep a record of work in progress and to work out piece work prices. C.F.W. Jones also took charge of the haulage engine department and received a salary of £165 a year. Phillips, C.F.W. Jones and Jenkinson, the Secretary who handled estimating, met the foremen weekly to review progress. By February 1912 the North British Engines were showing a margin of about 33 per cent on wages and materials to cover general expenses. Whilst this was below target, cash was soon to be received. The first engine had been delivered in March. A total of eleven engines had been supplied and £21,000 received by July and this had increased to £28,000 by October. Each engine cost £2,600.

Complications arose in November 1912, when C.F.W. Jones had a meeting with a representative from the North British. Cylinders had been supplied by the North British, which had not been constructed to the specification given to the Yorkshire Engine Co. Joints had been made with red lead rather than boiled oil. Reid, the North British locomotive engineer, visited Meadowhall the next day and agreed the

In 1914 the Yorkshire Engine Co. delivered five 0-6-0 goods locomotives to the Hull & Barnsley, the first order from that railway for seven years (YE1184). (LM p.4)

Yorkshire Engine Co. could use red lead. Reid also noticed his works had made mistakes with the stuffing boxes. Reid agreed his drawings were wrong and promised to sort things out. He did not wish failings by his men to cause further delays. He wanted to get deliveries back on schedule. He also told the Yorkshire Engine Co. that the engines already delivered were doing well.

The last of the North British Railways 4-4-2Ts had been delivered by January 1914. They had a boiler pressure of 175psi and weighed 68 tons 15cwt in working order. Designated as Class M by the North British Railway, the engines became Class C15 on grouping. They were known affectionately as the 'Yorkshire Tanks' or 'Yorkies' and were used initially on suburban services around Edinburgh and Glasgow and on the Clyde coast-stopping trains. Subsequently used more widely around Scotland, many were put into storage after nationalisation in 1948, but two survived in use on the Craigendoran-Arrochar push and pull service until April 1960.[4]

The Metropolitan Railway returned as a customer for new locomotives in 1912, although the Yorkshire Engine Co. had agreed to build six boilers for the Metropolitan for £499 each in 1910 and more boiler orders followed. The extent to which these 0-6-4Ts were designed by the Metropolitan's Chief Electrical and Locomotive Engineer Charles Jones is unclear. It seems likely that Jones did the outline designs, but the details were left to Harold Akroyd, the Chief Draughtsman of the Yorkshire Engine Co., and his team. The Yorkshire Engine Co. board minutes record that in August 1912 the Managing Directors, Jones and Moss, inspected the drawings prepared by Akroyd for the Metropolitan order and gave their approval. Akroyd was an able engineer and was to serve the Yorkshire Engine Co. for many years. A notebook in the archives in Sheffield records the prices he obtained in June 1907 for parts for the ill-fated motor project. His patents were used in the majority of haulage engines produced by the Yorkshire Engine Co.

The Metropolitan ordered a total of four 0-6-4Ts (YE 1283–4 and 1301–2). Categorised as Metropolitan Class G, the locomotives were not delivered till 1915–6. Numbered 94-96, the engines were also given names, with the first called *Lord Aberconway* in honour of the Chairman. No.95 was named *Charles Jones*. Although a report in the *Locomotive Magazine* implied this would be a large class, no more were built. Used for both goods and passenger traffic, they were the most powerful locomotives on the railway. Operating at a boiler pressure of 160psi, their weight in working order was 71 tons 1cwt.[5]

Orders for railways outside the UK were more limited in the period from 1906 to 1919. Amongst the most unusual locomotives were two 0-6-6-0Ts for the Nitrate Railways. These were not Fairlies, but a development of the articulated 'Meyer' type, which superseded the Fairlies on some of the railways in the nitrate fields. The two locomotives (YE 940–941) were used on the heavy inclines on the nineteen-mile stretch of line from the port of Iquique to Las Carpas. Weighing just less than 118 tons, they were capable of hauling 208 tons exclusive of their own weight at 8.5mph over an average gradient of 1:35. In places the line had a 1:21 gradient and the tightest curve was 300ft radius. The locomotives had two independently

Known as the Yorkshire Tanks at Cowlairs, this locomotive (YE1066) is the first of an order from the North British Railway for thirty 4-4-2Ts delivered in 1911–3; due to the Yorkshire Engine Co.'s cash shortage as a result of losses from its venture into car manufacturing, special payment terms had to be agreed. (LM p.5)

North British 4-4-2T (YE1073) continued in use on the Craigendoran-Arrochar push and pull service till April 1960. (Howard Turner Collection)

driven sets of six coupled wheels 3ft 9in in diameter. The rigid wheelbase was only 8ft 6in, but the total length over the buffers 35ft 8in. Exhaust steam passed out of a separate chimney located at the rear of the bunker. The locomotives were scrapped in 1931–2.[6]

A number of narrow-gauge locomotives were supplied to both UK and overseas customers. The Puerto Cabello & Valencia Railway bought a 3ft 6in-gauge 0-4-0ST with a working pressure of 150psi (YE 1096) in 1911 and Callenders Cable bought a similar-gauge 0-4-0ST in 1912 (YE1135). More unusual were a group of three 2ft-gauge 0-6-0Ts constructed for the public works department of the Indian State Railways in 1915. Weighing only 11 tons 2cwt, the side tanks held only 200 gallons of water and the bunker 8cwt. of coal. The cylinders were 8.5in in diameter. The locomotives were to be used on

Designed by C. Jones, Chief Mechanical Engineer of the Metropolitan Railway, the two 0-6-4Ts nos 94 (YE1283) and 95 were intended to enable the company to improve its services on the Aylesbury extension. Two more of the same class (nos 96 and 97) were built by the Yorkshire Engine Co. in 1916. (LM p.3)

construction work and had to be capable of drawing 80 tons up an incline of 1:100 on 18lb track at a speed of 8 to 10mph (YE 1285–1287).[7] An order for seven metre-gauge 0-4-4BTs for the South Indian Railway had been put in hand early in the war, but was postponed due to the war work priorities and the locomotives were not delivered till 1919 (YE 1288–1294).

The manufacture of industrial tank locomotives continued at modest levels. Seven 0-4-0STs were supplied to Goldendale Iron, Bolsover Colliery, Joseph Hardman, William Cooke, T.W. Ward and Hoyland Silkstone between 1907 and 1912. 0-6-0STs became more popular with eight built for Rothervale, Newbiggin, Midland Coal Coke & Tar, David Colville, Tirdonkin and Shirebrook between 1909 and 1917.

The production of boilers and the overhaul and repair of locomotives remained a main feature of the business up to and including the years of the First World War and for a time thereafter. Between 1906 and 1919 165 locomotive boilers were produced for the Indian State, Lancashire Derbyshire & East Coast, London Brighton & South Coast, West Galician, Metropolitan, Ottoman, South Eastern & Chatham, South African, Dublin & South Eastern, Taff Vale, West Clare and Nitrate railways, as well as for collieries and steelworks. With the locomotives for industry, the sale of a boiler was often part of a general overhaul of a locomotive. During the war locomotives were sent for overhaul by the Caledonian, Highland, London Brighton & South Coast and many others. Unlike some of the English railways, the Scottish companies maintained their normal colour schemes during the war. The Caledonian also made clear they did not want a plate fixed to the locomotive showing the Yorkshire Engine Co.'s name and the date of the repairs.[8]

Spares were made for the Yorkshire Engine Co. locomotives and for those made by other manufacturers. Sharp Stewart sent three tank engines for overhaul by the Yorkshire Engine Co. in 1907. South American railways such as the Buenos Ayres Great Southern, Buenos Ayres Western, Central Uruguay and Taltal regularly ordered spares during the period. For the Taltal fireboxes, throat and boiler plates were made for both Beyer Peacock and Kitson locomotives.

In spite of the problems with the motor car business, the Yorkshire Engine Co. board continued to look at new ventures, including one in the motor trade. In February 1910 a Mr Catton and a Mr Dutchman came to the board with designs for an 'anti-friction brake' for use on 20-30-ton and 15-2-ton trucks. By August the Yorkshire Engine Co. had built three sample sets of equipment, but Catton and Dutchman had disappeared and the venture folded. At the same time an 'oil engine' was built to

Orders for industrial-type tank engines were uncommon at this date; in 1911 the Puerto Cabello & Valencia Railway purchased a 3ft 6in-gauge 0-4-0ST (YE1096). (LM p.17)

Three diminutive 11-ton 2ft-gauge 0-6-0Ts (YE1285–7) were built for the Indian State Railways' United Provinces Public Works department for delivery in 1915; thereafter the Yorkshire Engine Co.'s locomotive production for India was suspended till after the war ended. (LM p.34)

Work on eight 0-4-4Ts for the South Indian Railway had to be postponed during the war and A36 (YE1288) was not delivered till 1919. (Peter Hawkins Collection)

the designs of a Mr Seeley and a Mr Wood. After initially blaming poor workmanship by the Yorkshire Engine Co., it was mutually agreed the engine would not work and, almost two years later, Seeley met his share of the costs.

The move into haulage engines for the mining industry was much more successful. Managed by C.F.W. Jones with the close involvement of Harold Akroyd, the Yorkshire Engine Co. draughtsman whose patents were used in many of the models, the first engines were delivered to the Chairman's colliery group, Rothervale, in May 1910. Rothervale continued to be a major customer for some years. Engines of various types were built including double drum, single drum and endless, all using an Akroyd patent on which he received a royalty. Over 100 had been sold by the start of the war in 1914. An agent was appointed specifically to sell to collieries, catalogues were produced and space taken in 1914 at the Manchester mining exhibition. Advertisements were placed in the *Colliery Guardian*. Sales of haulage engines continued till 1943 and brought useful spares business and other general colliery engineering work. In March 1914, for example, Rothervale ordered a single-deck pit cage to carry two tubs, alongside an order for haulage engines. C.F.W. Jones had been appointed a director in August 1913, following the death of the former Chairman, Emerson Bainbridge.

By the time the First World War broke out in 1914, the Yorkshire Engine Co. had struggled back to profitability. Profits exceeded £1,000 in 1910 and reached £12,077 in the year to December 1913, but there was still a debit balance on the profit and loss account of £8,742 and no prospect of a dividend for shareholders. In April 1914 a new General Manager, A.H. Gilling, was appointed on £500 a year plus a bonus of 5 per cent of profits. Willans, who had been Manager for a short period following Phillips departure, was offered a job under Gilling and accepted. A new Works Manager, Edwards, was recruited on £350 a year plus 1 per cent profit commission. In August Gilling wrote to the War Office offering to do war work.

The arrival of war created problems for the Yorkshire Engine Co. Men had left to join up, including C.F.W. Jones. Others had left to go to local works which were better equipped for armament manufacture and therefore able to pay higher wages. Money was tied up in the South Indian Railway order for seven 0-4-4Ts, which the Ministry of Munitions would not allow the Yorkshire Engine Co. to complete. The works remained old fashioned, even after some improvements in 1914. Economical gas engines had been bought to replace the steam engines which had provided power to the shafts in the works. Electric motors had been introduced for some tools and new lighting installed. The whole place had been whitewashed and the windows cleaned. Gilling noted it was not easy to convert locomotive engineers into shell makers. In 1917 an order was received from the Admiralty for watertight doors. In the same year the board debated building lavatories for female employees and a canteen. A new forge building was also constructed.

By December 1917 profits had reached £15,250 after bank charges and there was now a credit balance of £4,589. However, there was £16,500 outstanding on the preference shares before any dividends could be paid on the ordinary shares. The South Indian Railway locomotives were still not complete, so cash remained short. A year later profits were again up, but excess profits tax had to be paid of £13,595 from the profits for the year of £20,265. Turnover had reached £217,789, but the company had now to plan for the post-war period.

When the shareholders met in March 1920 to consider results for 1919, they were pleased with profits of £18,788, but cash was still short as work in progress was high and improvements had to be made to the plant. Some preference dividends had been paid out six months earlier, when payment for the seven South India locomotives had been received. Further dividends could not yet be contemplated. Eighty-seven men had served in the forces during the war. Eight had been killed and a roll of honour was erected in the works. Business looked to be good, as many companies had postponed other than essential repairs during the war. The Chairman had been made a baronet in May 1919 and was now Sir Frederick Jones, Bt.

The mining machinery business was sufficiently important to the Yorkshire Engine Co. to make it worth taking a stand at a mining exhibition in Manchester in 1913. (Sheffield Archives)

Apedale (YE1276) was one of two 0-6-0STs delivered to the Midland Coal, Coke & Iron Co. in 1915; the company purchased another 0-6-0ST, Knutton, in 1917. (LM p.19)

Above and below: *Two designs of haulage engine were illustrated in a Yorkshire Engine Co. catalogue produced after the First World War, when the haulage engine business was being developed by Captain Ward Jones. (Yorkshire Engine Co. Catalogue)*

Notes

1. The Yorkshire Engine Co. order book (YE1) shows YE 949–958 for the first ten chassis, YE 959–1008 for the next fifty chassis and YE 1009 for the six-cylinder chassis. The number of chassis completed cannot be readily established. The first ten were completed and subsequently modified. A figure of eighteen completed chassis was given at the March 1909 annual meeting, but it is not clear whether this is the number in stock in March 1909 or the total number completed to date, including those sold. More chassis were made in 1909–10 following the 1909 annual meeting, but the exact number is not recorded. Chassis production had ceased by August 1910.
2. According to Stephen Myers in *Cars from Sheffield*, 1986, the order was placed by the British & Colonial Mercedes Daimler Syndicate and royalties paid on the first fifty cars. No cars are believed to have survived.

Above: *No.24 (YE1277) was delivered during the early stages of the First World War to David Colville & Sons Ltd; but for the cab, the locomotive looks identical to YE1276. (LM p.11)*

Right: *Sir Frederick Jones, Bt, who with C.H. Moss took on the Managing Director role following the disastrous venture into car production, served as Chairman of the Yorkshire Engine Co. till June 1929. (Property of Sir Simon Benton Jones, Bt)*

3. Prices paid by the H&BR are quoted in www.lner.info for the Stirling LNER Q10 class (H&BR class A); *Locomotive Magazine*, July 1907, p.116.
4. *SLS Journal*, 'North British Railway 4-4-2 Tanks' by John T. Rutherford and A.H. McNair; *North British Railway* by Hamilton Ellis, p.203.
5. *Locomotive Magazine*, December 1915, Vol. XXI No.280.
6. *Locomotive Magazine*, September 1912, p.185; April 1952 p.127.
7. *Locomotive Magazine*, December 1915, p.266.
8. *SLS Journal*, March 1976, 'Some notes on the Yorkshire Engine Company' by C.B. Harley, p.76.

5

The Interwar Years
1919–1939

The period between the two world wars was challenging for the Yorkshire Engine Co. Work was short and prices low. The company could not escape the general recession of the late 1920s and early 1930s. In ten out of twenty years the business made a loss. All British locomotive builders suffered similar problems and had to rely largely on markets outside the UK. Britain's traditional overseas markets were now being entered by overseas suppliers. By 1930 Indian railways were placing 60 per cent of their orders in mainland Europe. South African and Egyptian railways were controlling their own affairs and buying at the cheapest price, which often meant outside the UK.

By the end of the period many locomotive builders had gone out of business. Hunslet Engine Co. had purchased the goodwill of Kerr Stuart in 1930 and the goodwill and drawings of Avonside in 1935. Financial incentives were provided in the Finance Act of 1935 to encourage rationalisation in the industry. Hawthorn Leslie merged with Robert Stephenson in 1937. Between 1937 and 1939 Armstrong Whitworth, Kitson and Nasmyth Wilson all ceased to manufacture locomotives, but the Yorkshire Engine Co. survived. The factories of Armstrong Whitworth and Nasmyth Wilson were taken over by the Government for the production of war materials.[1]

During the interwar period the Yorkshire Engine Co. designed and supplied a number of interesting locomotives, particularly to South America. As in earlier periods, its survival as a manufacturer of new locomotives was dependent on two or three larger customers, the most important of which was the Great Western Railway. The Yorkshire Engine Co. largely avoided experiments, although it did attempt to market a new design of steam tender locomotive. Industrial locomotives for collieries and steel works continued to be an important element of the business. Haulage engine orders for mining customers also held up, with about 600 supplied in the twenty-year period.

Gilling remained General Manager until August 1927, when to the board's regret he left for a better job. He had served the company since 1914. Sydney Jenkinson, who had been Company Secretary under Gilling, took over as General Manager. He was the son of H.C. Jenkinson, who had joined the company as an office boy in 1866 and had retired as Company Secretary in 1907. H.C. Jenkinson lived till 1928 and was therefore able to enjoy the satisfaction of seeing his son take the top post at the Yorkshire Engine Co. C.H. Moss, who had acted as Managing Director with Sir Frederick Jones in the aftermath of the motor venture, died in 1923. Sir Frederick continued as Chairman till June 1929 when his son, Charles Ward Jones, took over. Charles Ward Jones had served in the army during the First World War and risen to the rank of captain.

For a short period after the First World War, most of the Yorkshire Engine Co.'s railway and industrial customers had to catch up on repair work deferred during hostilities. The business was therefore sustained by repairs rather than by orders for new locomotives. The Taff Vale Railway ordered eleven boilers in February 1919 and the Barry Railway eight boilers the following month. The Barry Railway came back for a further twenty boilers and the Taff Vale another seven between 1921 and 1923. Following the acquisition of the Taff Vale by the GWR at the grouping in 1923, thirteen ex Taff Vale 0-6-2 tank engines were sent to Meadowhall in 1925–6 for rebuilding. The price for each engine was agreed once the locomotive had been stripped down. The GWR also ordered twenty boilers in 1925 and the Western Australian Government twenty in 1924.

Between 1925 and 1930 boiler orders declined, until the London North Eastern Railway produced an order for ten boilers for its Class J15 and J69 locomotives in 1930. In the period from 1919 to 1939 the Yorkshire Engine Co. produced a total of 184 boilers. Of these boilers over 100 were produced in the seven years immediately following the end of the First World War.[2]

In the first eighteen months after the war the Yorkshire Engine Co. sold spares to over forty different railways. As well as its traditional customers in South America, India, the UK and Ireland, spares were provided to railways in Spain, Burma, France, Portugal, Rhodesia, Nigeria and the Gold Coast (Ghana). In Spain boiler plates were supplied to the Chemin de Fer du Nord d'Espagne and copper plates and fireboxes to the Chemin de Fer Andalouse. The Puerto Cabello & Valencia also came back for spares. In the following eighteen months the Crown Agents added orders for railways in Cyprus, Uganda and Egypt. The Yorkshire Engine Co. continued to undertake general engineering work for local steelworks and collieries, an essential supplement to its railway business and the main reason for its survival in the Depression.

Once the seven 0-4-4Ts had been despatched to the South Indian Railway in 1919, no new locomotives were to leave Meadowhall till 1921. In that year locomotives were supplied to the Maryport & Carlisle Railway and to Babcock y Wilcox in Spain for the Northern Railway of Spain. Neither organisation appears to have had previous dealings with the Yorkshire Engine Co. In 1923 the Nitrate Railways returned with a significant order for six 4-8-4Ts. A year later the Bengal Nagpur ordered four 2-8-2s (YE1992–1995) and subsequently in 1932 five tenders were purchased. In 1925 an order was received for five 4-8-2s from the Central Railway of Peru. Orders were also received for standard industrial locomotives. When added to the buoyant boiler and spares business, the future for the company's locomotive manufacturing business looked reasonable in the early 1920s. Unfortunately this prosperity was not to continue.

The Maryport & Carlisle Railway was a forty-mile line built in the 1850s to connect the Cumbrian towns. Two 0-6-0s (YE1582–1583) were ordered in May 1919 and designed by the Yorkshire Engine Co. to meet the requirements of J.B. Adamson, the Locomotive Superintendent. The designs were recorded in the order book as being of the Hull & Barnsley type. Described in *The Locomotive* as 'good examples of the classical type of British six-coupled locomotive', they were said to give highly satisfactory service. With a working pressure of 170psi, saturated steam was distributed by Allan link motion. The total weight of engine and tender in working order was 89 tons 8 cwt.[3] According to C.B. Harley in his *Notes on the Yorkshire Engine Company*, the leading erector, Pat McNulty, stood admiring the first one and said 'She's worth all the trouble she's been'. The locomotives were delivered over Midland lines, where Adamson had once worked, using a very inadequate supply of unsuitable coal due to the miners' strike of 1921.[4]

The order from Babcock y Wilcox of Bilbao in Spain was a greater challenge. The contractor selected by Babcock was to supply a set of working drawings for a 4-8-0 express locomotive and to build the first engine. Babcock had secured an order for sixteen locomotives from the Northern Railway of Spain. This was Babcock's first locomotive order and the design was left largely to the Yorkshire Engine Co. The Spanish railways at the time were heavily graded and laid with light rails, which precluded the use of heavy axle loads. However, the railways were generally forward looking from a technical point of view. 'It was therefore to be expected that the conspicuous success of the three-cylinder locomotive in other lands should invite a trial of its potentialities in fulfilling the onerous requirements of the Spanish railways.'[5] The locomotive had to combine great power, light axle loads and the ability to generate abundant steam from poor-quality fuel.[6]

The 'Mastodon'-type 4-8-0 with an eight-wheeled tender (YE1658) was built to the 5ft 6in gauge. The combined weight of the locomotive and tender was 136.6 tons and the length over the buffers 76ft 2½in. A superheater designed by Babcock was used. The success of the first locomotive built by the Yorkshire Engine Co. was such that the subsequent fifteen were built by Babcock to identical design. The satisfaction of the Northern Railway of Spain resulted in Babcock receiving a follow up order for a number of 2-8-0s.[7] A contrasting view on the success of the 4-8-0s is given by L.G. Marshall in *Steam on the RENFE* where Marshall suggests the locomotives were poor steamers.[8] As far as the Yorkshire Engine Co. was

The Nitrate Railways were an important customer for spares up to 1950; the railway purchased a number of boilers both for Fairlies and other locomotives between 1890 and 1930. (Derek Penney Collection)

concerned, it was noted at a board meeting in August 1921 that the engine had contributed only £1,800 above labour and material costs. Babcock was asked for more and agreed to meet exchange rate losses, but not to increase the price. In September 1922 the Yorkshire Engine Co. received a considerable order from Babcock for wheels, axles, shafts, pistons, connecting and coupling rods for another six Mastodon 4-8-0s.

The last order the Yorkshire Engine Co. was to receive from the Nitrate Railways for new locomotives followed in November 1922. The two-cylinder 4-8-4Ts were said to be the heaviest tank engines in the world (YE 1941–1946) and cost £6,500 each. They weighed about 113 tons in working order. The order for the six locomotives was secured against fierce competition. Numbered 97 to 102, the engines were designed to fulfil the same task as the Meyer-type articulated locomotives supplied by the Yorkshire Engine Co. in 1908. They were said to be capable of hauling 180 tons up the incline to Las Carpas, slightly less tonnage than the Meyer-type 0-6-6-0s were supposed to draw up the same incline. Entering service on the Nitrate Railways in 1924, they had a working pressure of 180lb and the tractive force was 31,114lb at 75 per cent boiler pressure. The oil-fired locomotive carried 1,000 gallons of fuel and 3,400 gallons of water.[9] The locomotives were fitted with Westinghouse air brakes and 'Pyle' electric headlights. The Yorkshire Engine Co. had to provide one complete set of linen tracings, three sets of blueprints and three photographs.

The order for five 4-8-2 locomotives and tenders (YE2038–2042) for the Central Railway of Peru was placed by Sir Brodie Henderson of consulting engineers Livesey Son & Henderson on 24 February 1924. Delivery was to commence in forty-four weeks with a penalty for late delivery and the price was £8,500 each. The consulting engineers appear to have produced the basic design. The contract specified that the locomotives must not weigh more than 128 tons or 16 tons per wheel. The Central Railway of Peru was British-owned with 258 miles of track involving sixty-one bridges, sixty-six tunnels and twenty-one

YE made boilers of all sizes, as this photograph illustrates; the large boiler is for one of the 4-8-4T locomotives supplied to the Nitrate Railways of Chile in 1923-4 (YE 1941-6). The locomotives were shipped in parts and assembled on arrival. The smaller boiler has not been identified.

switchbacks. The section on which the Yorkshire Engine Co.'s locomotives were to serve rose from sea level to 15,865ft. There were seventy-five miles of continuous 4 per cent ruling gradients combined with uncompensated curves of 100m radius. The wheel base had to be very flexible and neither the leading nor intermediate wheels were flanged. To provide sufficient steam, the boiler was 6ft diameter with 200 brass tubes and twenty-two copper tubes. The weight was 123 tons 8cwt, well within the specified limit.[10] Unfortunately these locomotives proved to be unsatisfactory.

> In 1925 the Central experimented with some English Mountain-type engines which were almost if not quite a failure ... In spite of equalised suspension, adhesive weight on the drivers tended to bridge between the four-wheeled leading truck and the engine truck, making the locomotives so slippery that they could hardly get up the mountain at all if there were any damp or frost about![11]

The engines were converted to 4-8-0s by cutting a course out of the boiler.

Between 1922 and 1939 the Yorkshire Engine Co. produced a total of twenty-nine industrial tank engines. Fourteen were 0-6-0STs and nine were 0-4-0STs. The Yorkshire Engine Co. continued its standard practice of building industrial engines to stock. Where a purchaser was known, the engine would be built to the customer's choice of colour. Where no order had been received, engines would be finished in the Yorkshire Engine Co.'s distinctive livery. The body colour was a very dark blue. The cab, tank and bunker were lined out with a band of straw colour edged with light green.[12] The Yorkshire Engine Co. offered a number of standard locomotives for 2ft gauge and upwards. Immediately after the war the standard gauge 0-4-0 was normally offered with 12in by 18in or 14in by 20in cylinders and the 0-6-0 with 14in by 20in cylinders.[13]

The customers for industrial locomotives included many companies of the United Steel group, which had merged with the Yorkshire Engine Co. Chairman's company, Rothervale Collieries. The companies

One of four 2ft 6in-gauge 2-8-2s with six-wheel tenders (YE1994) for the Bengal Nagpur Railway despatched in 1924. (Derek Penney Collection)

One of two 0-6-0s (YE1582) designed by the Yorkshire Engine Co. to the specification of the Locomotive Engineer of the Maryport & Carlisle and delivered in 1921. (Peter Hawkins Collection)

4-8-0 three-cylinder tender locomotive for Babcock y Wilcox of Spain delivered in 1921 was described in the Yorkshire Engine Co. catalogue as 'one of the heaviest and most powerful engines ever built in Britain' (YE1658). (Silver Catalogue p.5)

included the Appleby Iron Co. (three 0-6-0STs YE2140-2142 for the new steel works), United Steel Rothervale (two 0-6-0STs to their specification, YE2240–2241) and Steel, Peech & Tozer (six 0-4-0STs in 1934–7, YE2343–5, 2361 and 2383–4). The Steel, Peech & Tozer locomotives were prepared to their own designs and weighed 43 tons 15cwt in working order. With 3ft 6in driving wheels and cylinders 16in by 22in, their tractive effort at 85 per cent was 20,517lb making them probably the most powerful 0-4-0s in the country. Special steel manufactured by United Steel was used in their construction.[14] These orders signified the growing links between the Yorkshire Engine Co. and United Steel, which were to culminate in the acquisition of the Yorkshire Engine Co. by United Steel after the Second World War.

Unlike some of its competitors the Yorkshire Engine Co. managed to obtain two orders in the period 1928–30 from two major UK railways, the LNER and the GWR. On 31 October 1927 the Yorkshire Engine Co. secured an order for nine 0-6-2Ts from the LNER. Gresley had considered a number of suburban tank designs in 1919 and had settled on the 0-6-2T configuration. The initial batches of these locomotives had been made at Doncaster and by the North British. The design had undergone several modifications by the time the Yorkshire Engine Co. secured its order (YE2220–2228). The first three were fitted with condensing gear for use on the Metropolitan line to Moorgate. The remaining six were non-condensing engines for use in the Southern Scottish area. The first three had vacuum brakes and the second six Westinghouse brakes. Working pressure was 170psi and weight in working order exceeded 70 tons.[15] The tractive effort was 19,945lb at 85 per cent boiler pressure. Forming part of the N2 class, the engines were largely withdrawn in the 1950s as diesels took over.

According to C.B. Harley, the steam test of one of these LNER locomotives contributed to the death of the erecting shop foreman. He had been confined to bed with a heavy cold, but insisted on coming down to the works to give the locomotive its usual tests. He drove the engine up and down the line in a howling wind and rain for several hours. When eventually he returned home from the draughty cab, his cold had become pneumonia and he died.[16]

'Believed to be the heaviest tank engines in the world' six 4-8-4Ts weighing 112 tons were delivered to the Nitrate Railways of Chile in 1923–4 (YE1945). (Derek Penney Collection)

The largest order the Yorkshire Engine Co. received in the period between the wars was for twenty-five Pannier tank engines from the GWR (YE2249–2273). The order was placed on 1 July 1929. Delivery had to start in twenty weeks and be completed in sixty weeks. As a result of this order, the Yorkshire Engine Co. delivered a total of twenty-six locomotives in 1930 and achieved a turnover of £126,000 and, for the first time since 1925, modest profits of £1,561. By the following year business had dropped away again with turnover falling to £42,000, only four locomotives delivered and losses of £1,046. The Yorkshire Engine Co.'s much larger rival Beyer Peacock also saw locomotive sales fall dramatically in the early 1930s. Beyer Peacock delivered ninety-six locomotives in 1930, forty-one in 1931 and twelve in 1932. In 1934 Beyer Peacock made only six locomotives.[17]

The twenty-five pannier tank engines supplied by the Yorkshire Engine Co. to the GWR were part of the 5700 class of 863 engines, which were introduced in 1929 largely for shunting and light goods duties. The first batches were made by the North British, W.G. Bagnall and Kerr Stuart and by the GWR itself at Swindon in 1929–30. The Yorkshire Engine Co. built numbers 6725–6749 largely in 1930. The class continued to be produced during and after the Second World War, with all the engines being made at Swindon from 1933 onwards. Like most railway companies the GWR took orders in-house as the recession deepened. Weighing about 49 tons and with a boiler pressure of 200psi, the locomotives were mostly withdrawn between 1957 and 1963. None of the Yorkshire Engine Co. engines have been preserved.

During the summer of 1922 General Manager Gilling started working with an inventive engineer, Edward Cecil Poultney, on the development of a new type of vacuum brake. Poultney was born in Ulverston in Lancashire in 1879 and served an apprenticeship with Vickers in Barrow in Furness. He went on to become a pupil of W. Pettigrew, the Engineer of the Furness Railway, and subsequently worked as a draughtsman and inspector of materials in the carriage and wagon department of the Furness. In 1906 Poultney joined the inspection staff of the consulting engineers, Messrs Rendel Palmer & Tritton. The Yorkshire Engine Co. met all the costs of developing the new brake. The board were, therefore, not prepared to see the patents registered, unless the Yorkshire Engine Co. participated in any revenue from the sale of the patent. After discussion it was agreed that Poultney should receive 75 per cent,

Five oil-fired 4-8-2s with double bogie tender, which were delivered to the Central Railway of Peru in 1925, were considered something of a failure (YE2042). (Jean Rose Collection)

YE1787 was supplied to the Hatfield Colliery in 1922 and became their No.2 locomotive; the photograph shows the 0-6-0ST awaiting steaming one Sunday in May 1964 at NCB Thorne Colliery. (Alec Swain – Transport Treasury)

This 0-4-0ST numbered 22 (YE2344) is one of three delivered to Steel, Peech & Tozer, a United Steel branch, in 1934 for the new Templeborough Rolling Mills. (Silver catalogue p.8)

Gilling 15 per cent and the Yorkshire Engine Co. 10 per cent of any revenues generated. Furthermore the Yorkshire Engine Co. should participate in manufacture of the products. Subsequently the Yorkshire Engine Co. decided it did not want to get involved with manufacturing the brakes.

Two years later in the spring of 1925 the company agreed to take out patent protection on an articulated locomotive design developed in conjunction with Poultney. Poultney wrote to the Yorkshire Engine Co. in April 1925 suggesting the patent should be in the joint names of himself, A.H. Gilling, H.A. Akroyd, who was still Yorkshire Engine Co.'s Chief Draughtsman, and the Yorkshire Engine Co. Gilling and Akroyd had both been involved in the design. Poultney wanted 2.5 per cent on the contract or selling price of new locomotives and 1.5 per cent on locomotives converted to his system. Patents were taken out in the UK, France, Germany, Belgium and the United States. The locomotives would be built by the Yorkshire Engine Co.

According to the brochure produced by the Yorkshire Engine Co. at the time, 'The Poultney Patent System' had two main objectives:

Nine 0-6-2Ts were built for the LNER in 1928–9; three were fitted with condensing gear for use on the Metropolitan Railway to Moorgate, of which 2684 (YE 2222) was the third; six were non-condensing for use in the Southern Scottish area. (Sheffield Archives)

The Yorkshire Engine Co.'s largest order between the wars was for twenty-five GWR 5700-class Pannier tanks; the locomotives were delivered in 1929–30. No. 6743 was YE2267. (Sheffield Archives)

1. *Increased power* in existing locomotives *with the same coal and water consumption.*
2. Locomotives of greatly *increased power over ordinary types with reduced coal and water consumption.*[18]

The patent was for an engine and tender unit, where the tender is equipped as a driving unit to complement the engine unit. 'The chief objective is to provide a locomotive which, for a given boiler capacity, will give a greater power without increasing the demand on the boiler and, at the same time, provide a locomotive which is flexible so that it can negotiate curved tracks and operate over roads requiring low axle loads.' Archibald Sturrock, who had introduced his steam tenders into the Great Northern Railway when working on the establishment of the Yorkshire Engine Co., might have been pleased that his rejected invention had come back in an improved form. To provide sufficient steam, Sturrock had designed locomotives with very large boilers and, as a result, high fuel consumption. Poultney's aim was to provide enough steam for the engine in the tender without having a very large boiler. In this way he hoped to reduce running costs and keep down the weight and axle loads of the main locomotive.

It was well appreciated by locomotive engineers at the time that a system which ensured that the maximum admission of steam would take place at about 50 per cent of the piston stroke would achieve considerable economy. By designing the cylinders to achieve a cut-off at about 50 per cent, as opposed to the more normal 80–90 per cent for freight locomotives, Poultney calculated that savings would be made, which would enable him to provide steam to the engine in the tender at no more than the normal cost of a freight locomotive. *The Locomotive* of 15 March 1926 summarised the benefits of the Poultney engines as follows:

> ...an economical type of motor giving exceptional starting power, a utilization of a high proportion of the combined engine and tender weight, means for distributing this weight over a large number of axles without complicated mechanism, a simple form of articulation involving no special pivots... and a convenient arrangement of working parts.

The article concluded by stating that the Yorkshire Engine Co. had the sole right to the invention.

Poultney and the Yorkshire Engine Co. put considerable effort into marketing the concept. A thirty-one-page brochure was printed incorporating a detailed explanation of the system, plus graphs and drawings of ten examples of 'Poultney' locomotives and two examples of tenders designed to be attached to existing locomotives. Discussions took place with the four UK railways following the grouping about a 4-8-2+0-8-0 design with UK clearances, but there was no interest. A 2-8-2+0-8-0 design for 5ft 6in gauge was also produced. Discussions took place with the Chemin de Fer du Nord and plans were made to convert an existing locomotive, but agreement could not be reached on price. Garratt-, Meyer- and Mallet-type locomotives were largely filling the need for which the Poultney design was intended. The lower first cost of a Poultney was insufficient to open up the market. Sturrock's failure was still remembered.

Eventually the Ravenglass & Eskdale Railway showed interest. The narrow-gauge Cumbrian Railway was an existing Yorkshire Engine Co. customer and had bought a boiler for its locomotive *River Irt* and six double bogie trucks for its freight services between April and June 1927. It agreed to have one of its engines modified to the Poultney design (YE2229). 2-8-2 *River Esk* had been built by Davy Paxman in 1923 to a design by Henry Greenly and was nominally a one-third scale model. A number of modifications were made to the boiler to suit the Poultney system. *River Esk* was returned to Ravenglass in 1928 as a 2-8-2+0-8-0, with cylinders 3 in by 8½in in the tender. The conversion was not a success and was considered to have insufficient steam. It may not, however, have been due to a fundamental flaw in the Poultney design. A new locomotive designed specifically to satisfy the Poultney system could well have performed better. In 1934 the locomotive reverted to its original form with a new tender. The original steam tender sat about unused until it was sent to Clarkson of York in 1966 to form the basis for the construction of another 2-8-2 locomotive, *River Mite*.

The Ravenglass & Eskdale was not the only UK narrow-gauge railway to pass business to the Yorkshire Engine Co. In 1931 the Romney, Hythe & Dymchurch Railway sent the parts for two 4-6-2s to be assembled by Yorkshire Engine. The boilers, constructed by Krauss of Munich, were received by the Yorkshire Engine

Left: *The cover of the impressive thirty-page brochure designed to promote the Poultney Patent steam tender locomotive, which was to be made solely by the Yorkshire Engine Co. (Derek Penney Collection)*

Below: *Poultney designs for 5ft 6in-gauge 2-8-2+0-6-0 and for standard-gauge 4-8-2+0-8-0 reproduced from the brochure in the March 1926 edition of Locomotive Magazine; in spite of considerable discussions in UK and Europe, neither locomotive was built. (LM, March 1926)*

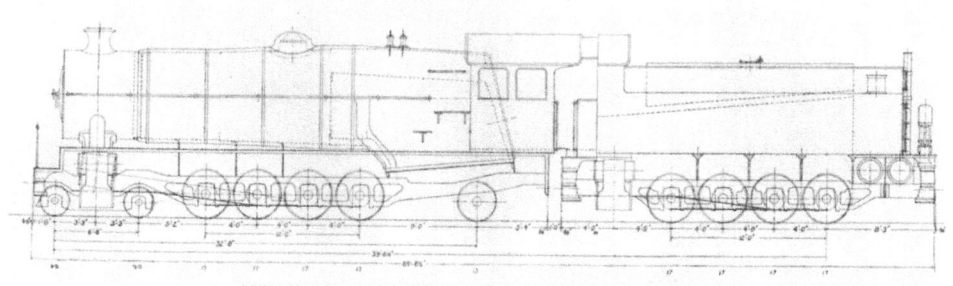

Opposite, bottom: *Both RH&DR miniature Pacific locomotives survive in 2008. Winston Churchill (YE2294), formerly called Dr Syn, enters New Romney station to pick up its train in the summer of 2007. (Author)*

Above: In 1928 the Yorkshire Engine Co. converted the Ravenglass & Eskdale Railway's River Esk from a 2-8-2 to a 2-8-2+0-8-0 by the addition of a Poultney patent steam tender (YE2229). It does not seem to have been any greater success than the Sturrock steam tenders on the Great Northern Railway in the 1860s. (Sheffield Archives)

Above: In 1931 the Yorkshire Engine Co. assembled two 4-6-2 Pacifics for the Romney Hythe & Dymchurch Railway. The parts for the locomotives were largely made by the railway itself or obtained from Germany. The Yorkshire Engine Co. made the whole of the tender. The photograph shows YE2294 as built. (Derek Penney Collection)

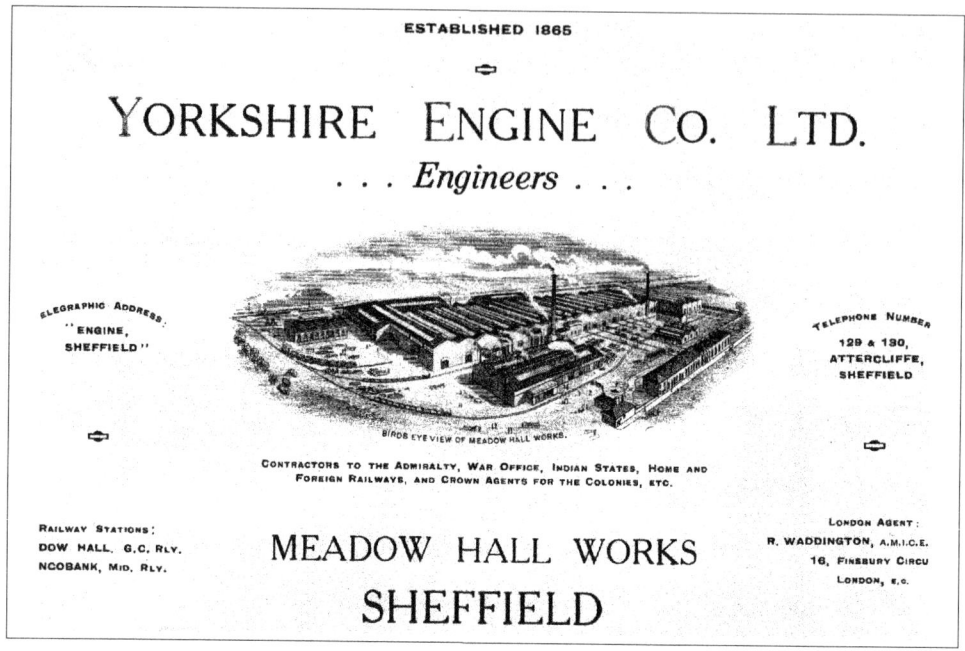

The illustration shown on the fly sheet of a 1930s catalogue gives the impression that Meadowhall was somewhat larger than in reality. (Derek Penney Collection)

Co. complete with clothing, sand boxes, smoke boxes and chimneys. YE made the tenders. Construction had been started by Davy Paxman, but some parts were made in the RH&DR workshops at New Romney. These two Canadian Pacific-type engines were, like the Ravenglass locomotives, built to a design by Henry Greenly. The first of the two locomotives (YE2294) was originally called *Doctor Syn*, after the fictional vicar of Dymchurch. It was renamed *Winston Churchill* in 1948. The second locomotive (YE2295) was originally called *Black Prince*, but was renamed *Dr Syn* in 1948, after the first *Dr Syn* was named *Winston Churchill*. Both locomotives have been subject to a number of modifications but continue in the RH&DR fleet today. At the time of writing in 2008 *No.9 Winston Churchill* is in regular use but *No.10 Dr Syn* requires an overhaul.[19]

The only overseas order for a new locomotive secured between 1925 and the start of the Second World War was an order for three diminutive 2-4-0Ts for the 2ft 6in-gauge section of the Eastern Bengal Railway (YE2320-2322). Delivered in 1932–3, the coupled wheels were 2ft ½in diameter and the cylinders 8½in by 12in. Working pressure was 150psi and the tractive effort at 85 per cent was 4,514. No.2320 survives on a plinth at the headquarters of the Eastern Railway in Calcutta.

The lack of overseas orders was not for want of effort. The board agreed to reduce the percentage applied to quotations for standing charges to make prices more competitive. The 80 per cent normally applied to railway orders was first reduced to 50 per cent and then on occasions to 40 per cent. Although the Yorkshire Engine Co. was sometimes the cheapest UK quote, orders increasingly went to continental suppliers. The Locomotive Manufacturers' Association (LMA), of which the Yorkshire Engine Co. was a member, laid down rules on pricing policy and the Yorkshire Engine Co. was not always free to reduce its prices unless other manufacturers agreed.

An illustrated catalogue describing the railway, mining and general engineering services on offer was produced in the 1930s. It included photographs of recent locomotives and haulage engines and of the machinery in use in the works. Attempts were made to get orders from Romania, China and Poland. Gilling visited Spain and Ireland to try and win business and Captain C.F. Ward Jones tried to obtain orders from Turkey. Boiler orders for India and Rhodesia were lost due to price. German locomotive builders

The heavy machine shop in the 1930s; the Cravens centre lathe of 1888 was capable of boring hollow shafts up to 60ft long and could have been used for gun barrels. Note the system for adjusting the lights. (Sheffield Archives)

were thought to receive Government subsidies, for their quotations were often below UK manufacturers' basic costs of production.

The LMA came forward with proposals for reducing the number of locomotive manufacturers in 1937 as the only way of saving some part of the UK private manufacturing business, since the four UK railways were largely building in their own workshops. One of the firms who took up the LMA's offer was Nasmyth Wilson. The company received £70,000 for its locomotive business in December 1937. It was able to continue its general engineering business, but had to hand over all its drawings, patterns and blocks relating to the building and repair of locomotives. The buy-out was funded by a levy of 3 per cent on the remaining members of the LMA.[20] The Yorkshire Engine Co. board discussed proposals to get out of locomotive building in June 1939 and were minded to accept a suitable offer from the LMA as in shareholders' interests. However, war intervened and no deal was completed.

There were further management changes in 1936, when Sidney Jenkinson died. He had been with the company for forty-eight years, a director for fifteen years and Managing Director and Secretary for ten years. The board decided to appoint the Chief Draughtsman, H.A. Akroyd, as joint general manager with W.H. Moore. Akroyd would look after men and technical matters and Moore commercial and secretarial affairs. Moore became ill in the following year and died. Akroyd was put in sole charge and in August 1938 was made a director. Captain Ward Jones normally took the chair at board meetings.

Business started to improve in the last quarter of 1936 and the year ended with a small profit of £942. Profits showed a more marked recovery in 1938, when £4,297 was made before depreciation. The profits had come from the general engineering business and the railway business made no contribution, but another war with Germany was expected. The Yorkshire Engine Co. had been appointed contractors to the Air Ministry in June 1939. The board agreed to invest in plant most suitable for its general engineering business.

Two of the forge men, with their white sweat towels, and a charge-hand rest on a pile of forgings in front of the boiler house. The forgings lie on the stone base once used for the steam engine which powered the line shafts, which drove the machinery in the works. (Sheffield Archives)

Notes

1. PEP Report on the Locomotive Industry, p.16.
2. *SLS Journal*, March 1976, 'Notes on the Yorkshire Engine Co.', p.76.
3. *The Locomotive*, September 1915, p.228; *Railway Gazette*, September 1921, p.379.
4. *SLS Journal*, March 1976, 'Notes on the Yorkshire Engine Co.', pp.76–77.
5. *The Locomotive*, February 1922, p.30; pp.29–31 provide a detailed description of the design features of this locomotive. The tractive force is not disclosed.
6. *The Locomotive*, March 1922, pp.61–64, includes cross sections through the boiler and through the firebox.
7. *The Locomotive*, March 1926, p.73.
8. *Steam on the RENFE* by L.G. Marshall 1965, p.172; it may be questioned how reliable Marshall's comments are since he did not seem to be aware that the Yorkshire Engine Co. made the first locomotive. The locomotives were still in use in 1964.
9. *The Locomotive*, May 1932, 'The Nitrate Railways and its locomotives', p.161; see also C.P. Harley's *Notes on the Yorkshire Engine Company*, p.79.
10. *The Locomotive*, June 1925, p.172–3, and June 1925, pp.180–183.
11. *Railways of the Andes*, Brian Fawcett, p.36; Fawcett joined the Central in 1924 and worked in the Locomotive department for many years, where he rose to the rank of Assistant Chief Engineer.
12. *Notes on Yorkshire Engine Company* by C.B. Harley, *SLS Journal*, p.75.
13. Undated Yorkshire Engine Co. catalogue; the locomotives used to illustrate the catalogue were produced on or before 1914. It seems likely the catalogue was issued immediately after the war when locomotive manufacturing was restarted in 1920.
14. *SLS Journal*, December 1948 – members' visit to Steel Peech & Tozer – and Vol.17, 1946, p.239; *Railway Modeller* February 1979, p.52; *The Locomotive*, February 1935, p.36.
15. The *Locomotive*, November 1928, p.345.
16. 'Notes on Yorkshire Engine Company' by C.B. Harley, *SLS Journal*, p.84.
17. *Beyer Peacock*, R.L. Hills and D. Patrick, pp.175–176.
18. *The Poultney Patent Locomotive*, a 31-page brochure produced by the Yorkshire Engine Company, p.3.
19. More information is available on www.rhdr.org.uk.
20. *Nasmyth Wilson & Co.* by John Cantrell, pp.106–7.

6

Second World War and the End of Steam 1939–1956

In contrast to the First World War, the Government gave more positive support to locomotive production and maintenance in the Second World War. Although the Yorkshire Engine Co.'s output of new locomotives and boilers was small, maintenance of locomotives to keep local collieries and steelworks operational was critical to the war effort. Once the war was drawing to an end, the Yorkshire Engine Co. board had to think of the future. An offer from United Steels in 1945 provided the shareholders with an acceptable opportunity to divest. The plant was old and needed complete refurbishment. It was already clear to some that diesel locomotives were likely to replace steam and the Yorkshire Engine Co. had not the resources on its own to adapt to the changing market. A decision to make diesel locomotives was taken in 1948. The last steam locomotive left Meadowhall in 1956.

Much of the Yorkshire Engine Co.'s general engineering work in connection with the war effort came via two major local firms Thomas Firth & John Brown and Steel, Peech & Tozer, the latter a United Steel branch. These two firms plus Firth Vickers Stainless and John Thorneycroft sub-contracted Admiralty work to the Yorkshire Engine Co. throughout the war. Items were made for destroyers, cruisers and other Naval vessels including carrier rails, guide rails, studs, washers and nuts. Crank shafts were forged and rudder stocks machined. Rough-hewn gun barrels were sent by the Ministry of Supply to the Yorkshire Engine Co., where the workforce had to bore a hole through the centre. The machinery was still belt driven from a shaft running down the shop from a single gas engine. Even the machine for putting teeth in the rack rails was found useful in the war.[1] The gun barrel business was to continue after the war, but with more modern machinery.

Meadowhall was kept busy with locomotive overhauls predominantly for steelworks and collieries. Often the work to be done was extended once the locomotive had been stripped down. One of the first locomotives to be overhauled in 1939 was *Victoria*. She was the first 0-4-0ST built by the Yorkshire Engine Co. and supplied to Earl Fitzwilliam collieries in 1869 (YE118). The locomotives put in for overhaul were made by a wide range of manufacturers including Avonside, Bagnall, Andrew Barclay, Manning Wardle, Hudswell Clarke, Hunslet, Robert Stephenson and Hawthorn Leslie. Many of the locomotives from two United Steel steelworks, Steel Peech & Tozer and Appleby Frodingham, were sent in succession for repair to the Yorkshire Engine Co., as well as locomotives from the United Steel-owned Rothervale Collieries. Some customers bought locomotive parts to do the repairs themselves and others might remove a boiler from its frame and send it to Meadowhall for refurbishment. Yorkshire Engine Co. fitters would be sent out to local works to repair locomotives in the customer's plant, taking the necessary parts with them.[2]

The locomotive overhaul business continued to be an important source of revenue after the war, as companies sought to catch up on a backlog of repairs. Specifications could be detailed, as in the case of a Nunnery Colliery locomotive in August 1946:

> Cut out existing firebox together with fire hole and foundation rings, also 146 tubes and fit new copper firebox including 146 new tubes ... Supply a new firebox riveted up with copper rivets, the plate being ½in thick with the exception of the tube portion of the tube plate which should be ¹³⁄₁₆th in thick; fitting to the existing shell together with the old foundation and fire hole ring...

Appleby Frodingham's No. 11 locomotive, an 0-6-0ST made by Hawthorn Leslie, was overhauled at Meadowhall in 1946. (Derek Penney Collection)

Delivery was to be in eleven months, because of a shortage of copper plates, which would not be available for nine months.

Orders for boilers and haulage engines did not approach the levels achieved in the 1920s. The first overseas orders for two boilers during the war came from the Jodhpur Railway followed by an order for five from the Rohlikund & Kumaon Railway. Predominantly local customers bought a total of nine boilers between 1941 and 1946. Only nine new haulage engines were supplied, although orders for spares and overhauls were again important. The last haulage engine was supplied in 1943. Of the nine supplied during the war, six went to United Steel's Rothervale Collieries.

The Yorkshire Engine Co. made only six new locomotives between 1939 and 1945. An 0-4-0ST was supplied to Sheffield Corporation Electricity department with 3ft 3in wheels and with cylinders 12in by 20in in 1941 (YE2403) and a similar locomotive to Steetley Lime & Basic in 1942. This locomotive (YE2407), named *June*, had 14in by 20in cylinders. Three electric locomotives were assembled by the Yorkshire Engine Co. on behalf of Clayton Equipment. A four-wheeled battery electric locomotives was supplied to Capenhurst Ordnance Factory in 1941 (YE2404) and a four-wheeled electric trolley to Warwickshire Electricity (YE2411). ICI Billingham also bought an electric trolley in June 1944. Yorkshire Engine Co. made the mechanical parts and provided facilities for Capenhurst to install the electrics. The Yorkshire Engine Co. then painted and numbered the vehicles. The sixth new locomotive was purchased by Sheepbridge Coal & Iron in 1943 (YE2413). This was a 0-6-0ST with 3ft 5in driving wheels and 16in by 22in cylinders.[3] It was ordered by the Ministry of Supply Iron & Steel Control in connection with a new calcining scheme. No further new locomotives were supplied until 1947.

Like the other remaining UK locomotive manufacturers, profits were satisfactory during the war years; they exceeded £6,000 every year from 1939 to 1943. There was cash in the bank, although provision had to be made for 'excess profits' tax imposed during the war and funds were spent on improvements to the works, including new lighting. As a result of the improved financial position, the board decided that some dividends could be paid to preference shareholders, who had received nothing

One of the few locomotives built during the Second World War was June, a 0-4-0ST for Steetley Lime & Basic (YE2402). (Derek Penney Collection)

Another wartime product was this electric trolley locomotive for ICI; completed in 1944, YE2414 was assembled at Meadowhall for Clayton Equipment. (Derek Penney Collection)

since 1928. Two years of preference dividends were paid in 1940 and two more in 1942. Profits in 1944 were just below £6,000, but still sufficient to pay preference dividends up to December 1937. Ordinary shareholders continued to receive nothing. The board told shareholders at the May 1941 annual meeting that 'very useful work has been done in the common cause'. Some bomb damage had been experienced but this had not disrupted output.

Even whilst the war continued, thoughts were being given to the future for locomotive manufacturing. A meeting was held at the LMA offices in late 1943, but nothing appears to have come from it, although Hawthorn Leslie decided to pull out of locomotive manufacture in 1944. More importantly Captain Ward Jones, who was on the United Steel board, told the Yorkshire Engine Co. board in December 1943 that United Steel was considering standardising their locomotives and he would let the Yorkshire Engine Co. board know when matters were clarified. At the same meeting Akroyd was thanked for his tireless efforts running the business. It was noted that very few staff had less than thirty years of service and some had been with the business as much as fifty years.

The May 1944 general meeting of shareholders was to be the last independent Yorkshire Engine Co. meeting. By the time of the next meeting in July 1945, the Yorkshire Engine Co. was a branch of the United Steel Companies. A Yorkshire Engine Co. board meeting was held in April 1945 to pay the outstanding dividends on the preference shares. A final meeting was held on 29 June 1945, when 2,137 ordinary shares and 5,611 preference shares were transferred to United Steel. Sir Walter Benton Jones, Chairman of United Steel and Captain Ward Jones's brother, was elected a director, and Gerald Steel, also on the United Steel board, joined the Yorkshire Engine Co. board.

Sir Walter Benton Jones appears to have been the prime mover behind the acquisition of the Yorkshire Engine Co. by United Steel. Sir Walter had advanced the proposal to the United Steel board that all the engineering workshops in a steelworks should be brought together in a single location, rather than dispersed around the works, as was the current custom. He considered that the Yorkshire Engine Co. would meet the need for a central engineering workshop in the Sheffield area for the two local works, Steel Peech & Tozer in Rotherham and Samuel Fox in Stocksbridge.[4] Such a workshop might also undertake some outside contracting. This concept was subsequently abandoned, but Yorkshire Engine Co. was retained to manufacture and repair locomotives. By March 1945 United Steel's offer was accepted by 97 per cent of the Yorkshire Engine Co.'s shareholders. The cost to United Steel was £82,800. In addition United Steel set aside £100,000 to reequip the Yorkshire Engine Co. Although this was a large sum by Yorkshire Engine Co. standards, it was a modest sum for United Steel, which had plans for £16.8 million of capital expenditure at the time.[5]

With the acquisition of the Yorkshire Engine Co. by United Steel, there were inevitable management changes. Harold Akroyd, who had been with the Yorkshire Engine Co. for over forty years and General Manager since 1937, retired in 1948 when he reached the age of sixty-five. The technical and plant management aspects of his role were taken on by a very experienced engineer, Joseph Compton. Compton had been educated at Marlborough College and, after a period of service with the RAF in the First World War, undertook a privileged apprenticeship with Beyer Peacock. Once his training was complete, he joined the Great Indian Peninsular Railway as a draughtsman and worked his way up to Chief Mechanical Engineer of the railway in 1945. He joined the Yorkshire Engine Co. in April 1948 at the age of forty-seven and retired with the closure of the works in 1965.[6] The General Management role was taken by a man named Col. Banks, who served with the Yorkshire Engine Co. till 1954–5. Banks is said to have been somewhat short-tempered. Employees were advised to stand well back as Banks passed head down with his hands in his pockets kicking doors open as he went. He encouraged the formation of trades unions in the works and would only discuss pay issues with the union representative. He was responsible for having a canteen installed. Known as the 'Yorkshire Engineer', it was run by a lady named Blossom.[7] Banks appears to have fallen out with United Steel's top management over an American piece work system, which he feared would threaten quality standards.[8]

United Steel had conducted a survey in 1944, which showed the company had 140 locomotives. The engineers responsible for each works were asked to consider standardisation. However, it was not until

Sir Walter Benton Jones, the eldest son of Sir Frederick and the architect of the purchase of the Yorkshire Engine Co. by United Steel. (Property of Sir Simon Benton Jones, Bt.)

May 1946 that a paper was presented to the United Steel board, which showed United Steel would need forty-two new locomotives over the next ten years. Twenty-two would be required on or before 1951 and the remaining twenty by 1956. Five different standard types of locomotive were envisaged with 0-6-0s predominating. Whilst orders from United Steel would provide a useful base load, a total of forty orders over ten years would not keep Meadowhall busy.[9]

The first United Steel orders were placed with the Yorkshire Engine Co. in 1945. Delivery times were typically twelve to fourteen months and were influenced as much by availability of steel and other raw materials as by works capacity. The most popular locomotive supplied to United Steel subsidiaries was a Type I 0-6-0ST with 16in by 24in cylinders and 3ft 8in wheels. The Type I weighed about 50 tons and was built to a United Steel specification. The budget cost of one of these engines in 1947 was £8,194. The budget for a more modest Type IV 0-4-0ST was £5,031.[10] Types IV and V were both 0-4-0STs, but cab dimensions, cylinder size, grate area, water and fuel capacity were all greater in the Type V than the Type IV version.

Whilst the Type IV was a Yorkshire Engine design, the Type I was a copy of a Robert Stephenson locomotive. When Appleby Frodingham placed their order for the first Type I on 20 November 1945, the Yorkshire Engine Co. was instructed to build the locomotive:

> ... in accordance with their standard specification enclosed. We are particularly to note the modifications at the end of the specification. The locomotives are to be *replicas* (author's italics) of their existing (Stephenson) locomotives of this size ... materials and workmanship throughout to be of a first class order and equal to main line practice.

YE2423 was the second of two Type I 0-6-0STs completed for the Appleby Frodingham branch of United Steel in 1947. (Derek Penney Collection)

The Yorkshire Engine Co. already had a sound knowledge of the Stephenson locomotives, for several Appleby Frodingham locomotives had been overhauled at Meadowhall in recent years. It is not clear whether the Yorkshire Engine Co. obtained copies of Stephenson's drawings or had to prepare their own. The head of the Yorkshire Engine Co. drawing office in the 1950s was Alf Wood, an ex-Robert Stephenson employee, who may have been employed in 1945. When the second order for Type Is was entered in the drawing office order book, the locomotives were described as being of the 'Stephenson pattern'.

Between 1947 and 1951 the Yorkshire Engine Co. made a total of thirty locomotives for United Steel branches. The standard specifications for both Type I and Type IV were modified for subsequent orders in the light of experience or to suit the circumstances of a particular works. There were, for example, modifications to the shape of the cab and the smoke box of the second three Type I locomotives delivered to Appleby Frodingham in the light of experience with the first two:

UNITED STEEL ORDERS 1947–1951

Branch	YE Number	Delivery Date	Wheel Arrangement	Type	Customer Number
Appleby Frodingham	2422	1947	0-6-0	I	27
Appleby Frodingham	2423	1947	0-6-0	I	28
Workington Harbour & Docks	2425	1947	0-4-0	V	1
Appleby Frodingham	2426	1948	0-6-0	I	29
Appleby Frodingham	2427	1948	0-6-0	I	30
Appleby Frodingham	2428	1948	0-6-0	I	31
Workington Iron & Steel	2429	1948	0-4-0	IV	17
United Steel Ore Frodingham	2433	1948	0-6-0	I	7

Customer	YE Number	Delivery Date	Wheel	Type	Customer Number
Appleby Frodingham	2434	1948	0-6-0	I	16
United Coke & Chemicals	2435	1948	0-4-0	IV	2
United Coke & Chemicals	2438	1949	0-6-0	I	1
Appleby Frodingham	2439	1949	0-6-0	I	34
Samuel Fox	2440	1949	0-6-0	I	4
Appleby Frodingham	2442	1949	0-6-0	I	66
Steel Peech and Tozer	2475	1949	0-4-0	V	30
Appleby Frodingham	2476	1949	0-6-0	I	21
Appleby Frodingham	2477	1949	0-6-0	I	5
Appleby Frodingham	2478	1949	0-6-0	I	15
Samuel Fox	2479	1949	0-6-0	I	6
United Steel Ore Exton[11]	2483	1950	0-6-0	I	39
United Steel Ore Exton	2484	1950	0-6-0	I	37
Samuel Fox	2485	1950	0-6-0	I	10
Appleby Frodingham	2486	1950	0-6-0	I	2
United Steel Ore Frodingham	2487	1950	0-6-0	I	7
Appleby Frodingham	2488	1950	0-6-0	I	25
United Steel Ore Exton	2489	1950	0-6-0	I	36
Samuel Fox	2498	1951	0-6-0	I	9
United Steel Ore Frodingham	2500	1951	0-6-0	I	15
United Steel Ore Exton	2501	1951	0-6-0	I	27
United Steel Ore Exton	2502	1951	0-6-0	I	33

With thirty locomotives acquired by United Steel in the five years to 1951, actual numbers exceeded the original plan numbers by ten. This was fortunate for the Yorkshire Engine Co. for in the same five-year period the Yorkshire Engine Co. supplied only six industrial locomotives to third parties. The nationalisation of the coal industry in 1946 took the Rothervale Collieries out of United Steel and reduced the opportunity for orders from this source. In the five years to 1951 five 0-4-0STs were sold to the National Coal Board (NCB) and a single 0-6-0ST to Lancashire Steel. This locomotive was said to be the best steam locomotive in the works at the time.

OTHER LOCOMOTIVE ORDERS 1948–1951

Customer	YE Number	Delivery Date	Wheel	Type	Customer Number
National Coal Board Northern Division	2430	1948	0-4-0	IV	Risehow 1
National Coal Board Northern Division	2431	1948	0-4-0	IV	St Helens 2
National Coal Board Northern Division	2432	1948	0-4-0	IV	Moresby 4
National Coal Board Barnsley Area	2473	1949	0-4-0	V	York 2
National Coal Board Barnsley Area	2474	1949	0-4-0	V	York 1
Lancashire Steel Irlam	2499	1951	0-6-0	I	24

This photograph of YE2425 for Workington Harbour & Docks Board was used to illustrate a Type V 0-4-0ST in the Yorkshire Engine Co. catalogue of about 1951/2. (Derek Penney Collection)

YE2483 was one of a batch of six Yorkshire Engine Co. Type I 0-6-0s built to stock all of which went to United Steel branches. This locomotive went to the ore mining branch at Exton Park, where it is still at work in March 1961. (Alec Swain – Transport Treasury)

A Stephenson look-alike Type I was said to be the best steam locomotive at Lancashire Steel Corporation's Irlam works (YE2499). (Derek Penney Collection)

United Steel orders were to be the sole source of orders from industrial users in the final four years of steam locomotive production. Another twenty-two saddle tanks were supplied to United Steel subsidiaries between 1952 and 1955. These included ten Type Is, four Type V 0-4-0STs and eight 'Austerity' 0-6-0STs.

The 'Austerity' locomotives (YE2566–2573) were a wartime standard design based largely on Hunslet Engine Co. practice. Locomotives of the Austerity design were built for the Ministry of Supply by many leading manufacturers, but not the Yorkshire Engine Co., during the war. Austerities continued in production after the war with the last 'Austerity' delivered by Hunslet to the NCB in 1964. The eight Yorkshire Engine Co. 'Austerity' 0-6-0STs were built in 1954. Some boilers and other parts came from Hunslet. Externally the Yorkshire Engine Co. 'Austerities' were identical to others, with the exception of wheel centres, which were twelve spoke and made of steel rather than the conventional fourteen spoke made of iron, and the buffers, which were oval.[12] The Yorkshire Engine Co. had had some previous experience with 'Austerity' locomotives in 1950, when nine had been stripped and re-assembled for the Ministry of Supply. It is not clear whether the eight Austerities were made by the Yorkshire Engine Co. solely because the locomotives were for a United Steel subsidiary or whether the manufacture of the eight 'Austerities' was somehow tied into another deal under which the Yorkshire Engine Co. took over Western Region Pannier tank orders from Hunslet.[13] The eight 'Austerities' were for the United Steel ore mining branch's operations at Frodingham in Lincolnshire and Exton Park in Rutland.

Of the industrial locomotives made by the Yorkshire Engine Co. between 1947 and 1955, three survive in 2007. The oldest and sole surviving Type V 0-4-0ST (YE2474) spent its working life with the NCB near Barnsley and is now awaiting restoration at the Embsay & Bolton Abbey Railway. The other two survivors are both Type I 0-6-0STs. YE2498, which was supplied to Samuel Fox in 1951, is on view at the Buckinghamshire Railway Centre, where it awaits the removal of asbestos lagging. YE2521 was one of four 0-6-0STs supplied to Appleby Frodingham in 1952 and is at present based at Barrow Hill Roundhouse, near Chesterfield for repair. It is owned by the National Mining Museum.

The Yorkshire Engine Co. would not have been able to survive during its final steam years without substantial work from British Railways Western Region. General Manager Banks is said to have run through the works announcing the business was saved, when the order was received for thirty Pannier

Another Type I at United Steel's Exton Park in March 1961, No.26 (YE2512) was delivered in 1952. (Alec Swain – Transport Treasury)

Probably the last Type I 0-6-0ST is under construction in the erecting bay at Meadowhall, with parts in the bay behind ready for the construction of an Austerity 0-6-0 for United Steel's ore mining branch at Exton Park. The erector standing just to the left of the steam dome is Pat McNulty, then aged about seventy. (Sheffield Archives)

The Yorkshire Engine Co. built eight Austerity locomotives for United Steel's ore mining branch. This July 1963 photograph shows one of the Austerities YE2572 alongside a later Janus YE2897. (Roger Monk)

Austerity 75072, one of thirty built by Robert Stephenson & Hawthorns in 1943, is undergoing an overhaul at Meadowhall. (B.N. Collins)

One of the few Yorkshire Engine Co. industrial steam locomotives still surviving in the UK, YE2498 is photographed at Buckingham Rail Centre at Quainton Road in June 2007; it awaits removal of asbestos lagging. The locomotive is another Type I delivered to United Steel's Samuel Fox branch in 1951. (Author)

YE2521 is another Yorkshire Engine Co. steam survivor; photographed under repair at Barrow Hill Roundhouse in August 2006, it was supplied initially to Appleby Frodingham and then used by the National Coal Board. (Howard Turner)

tanks on 5 February 1948. A tender for this order had been submitted on 21 August 1947. The order for the GWR Class 9400 Pannier tank engines transformed the revenue of the business, as the figures below illustrate. The table appears to have been prepared for the Yorkshire Engine Co. Chairman in September 1950.

Activity	Nos of Items	1948/9 Revenue £	Nos of Items	1949/50 Revenue £
New Locomotives	11	78,902	19 incl. 12 GWR Pannier Tanks	171,361
Repaired Locomotives	8	37,015	5	20,286
New Boilers	3	4,457	1	1,678
Repaired Boilers	4	5,075	6	8,137
General Machining	-	54,846	-	61,751
Forging	-	8,155	-	30,163
	Total	188,450	Total	293,376

To accommodate the growth in the business, numbers employed rose. The workforce of 343 in June 1948 increased to 396 by June 1949 and to 424 by June 1950. The company remained a family oriented business, with two generations of a family often working at the Yorkshire Engine Co. together. It was easier to get a job at the Yorkshire Engine Co. if a would-be employee had a father or other family member working there. Pat McNulty, who was the senior fitter responsible for the Nitrate Railways locomotives in 1923 (YE1941–1946) and received the MBE, worked at Meadowhall with his two sons, Joe and Donald. Pat was so highly regarded that he retired one Friday and returned the following Monday. He was still employed in 1952 aged seventy. The family spirit was fostered by works dances and other social events at the Wincobank Social Club. Competitions for darts, cricket and fishing encouraged friendly rivalry between departments. Football was played at Concord Park. There was an annual outing for the whole family to the coast.[14]

However, the issue which preoccupied Compton and his senior colleagues at this time will have been the move into diesel production and the impact on the workforce. United Steel's Works Managers' conference had discussed the use of diesel locomotives in steel works in December 1946 and agreed it was desirable to try one at either the Steel Peech & Tozer plant at Templeborough or at Workington in Cumbria. An order was placed with the Yorkshire Engine Co. by Steel Peech & Tozer for two diesel locomotives on 6 July 1948. The first two diesels were not to be delivered for over two years. During this period the works was totally refurbished. The manufacture and repair of steam locomotives and the provision of spares had to continue during the refurbishment, as well as preparations for the manufacture of diesel locomotives. Modern machinery driven by individual electric motors replaced most of the belt-driven machinery and a concrete floor was installed. Where belt-driven machines were retained, small sections of the old shaft were operated by electric motors. At least one slot-drilling machine dated 1865 was still in use after the refurbishment.

The initial 1948 order for thirty GWR 9400 Class Pannier Tanks for British Railways Western Region was supplemented by an order for two further batches of ten in 1950. British Railways had placed an order for twenty locomotives with Hunslet at much the same time as it placed the order for thirty with the Yorkshire Engine Co. By Christmas 1950 Hunslet had a substantial backlog of orders and was embarrassed that it would not be able to deliver its order for twenty in the foreseeable future. It therefore arranged to subcontract the order for the twenty Pannier tanks to the Yorkshire Engine Co. It may be that the supply of the eight 'Austerities' to United Steel's ore mining branch was also linked to Pannier tank deal.[15]

The original thirty Pannier tanks had Yorkshire Engine Co. works numbers 2443–2472 and were delivered between 1949 and 1952 and became Western Region numbers 8450–8479. The additional

The Yorkshire Engine Co.'s first diesel for Steel, Peech & Tozer was YE2480. It survives at Peak Rail in Derbyshire in December 2007. (Author)

Machine shop following re-equipment in 1951. Machines driven by electric motors have largely replaced the old shaft-driven machinery and new floors have been laid. (Blue catalogue p.2)

The final steam locomotive to be built by the Yorkshire Engine Co. left the works in September 1956. YE2584 was the last of fifty Pannier tanks built by the Yorkshire Engine Co. after the Second World War, of which the final twenty including this locomotive had been built under a subcontract from Hunslet. (Jean Rose Collection)

twenty Pannier tanks had both Hunslet and Yorkshire Engine Co. works numbers and incorporated many parts made by Hunslet. The works numbers for the additional twenty were YE2544–2553 and YE2575–2584 and Hunslet 3720–3739. The first ten of the second order were delivered in 1954–5 and became Western Region 9490–9499. The final ten were delivered in 1955–6 and were given Western Region numbers 3400–3409. Pannier tank No.3409 was despatched on 25 September 1956 and was the last new steam locomotive to leave Meadowhall. The Yorkshire Engine Co., therefore, made a total of fifty of the 210 Pannier tanks in the 9400 Class. To ensure a good standard of work, a team of six fitters was given the task of constructing each locomotive. Pat McNulty was responsible for setting up the valves and took pride in the fact that it was only Yorkshire Engine Co.-made Pannier tanks which did not need to have their valves reset on arrival at Swindon.[16] Although two of the class survive, neither was made by the Yorkshire Engine Co.

The Yorkshire Engine Co.'s new locomotive production in the final steam years was not confined to the manufacture of industrial and Pannier tanks for UK customers. Five locomotives were supplied to South America. The first in 1952 was a modified Type I 0-6-0ST for the Peruvian Corporation, a British-owned company, which operated over 1,000 miles of line in Peru. The locomotive (YE 2511) was ordered in 1951 and despatched in 1952. It was designed to burn oil and had centre couplers and a brass Klinger water gauge. In addition a total of four locomotives were supplied to two railways, the Central Railway of Paraguay and the Chilean Northern, part of the metre gauge Antofagasta (Chile) & Bolivia Railway, an old Yorkshire Engine Co. customer.

In May 1951 the Yorkshire Engine Co. received an order via The English General Agency on behalf of the Central Railway of Paraguay for two 2-6-0s. These locomotives were based on a 1910 North British Locomotive Co. design. The British-owned railway's main line ran from the Paraguayan capital of Asuncion to Encarnacion, where a train ferry crossed the River Alto to connect with the Argentine Northern Railway. The railway had about 275 miles of track including a number of branches. The locomotives

YE2584 is surrounded by the erecting shop workforce. On engine: unidentified and Denis Potts. Centre row, left to right: unidentified slinger, Arnold Algar, Gordon Birdall, Terry Goddard, Neil Winkle, unidentified riveter, Harry Draycott, Ken Thompson, unidentified, Frank Webster, John Edwards, Pete Jackson, George Lawless senior, John Christmas, unidentified, Charlie Timms, Bernard Ledger, unidentified, Harold Prince. Front row: Lewis Fernley, unidentified, Mac Clark, Duncan Fernley, Nat Bilby, Frank Walker, Ken Hayter. (John Christmas Collection)

were to haul 520-ton passenger and goods trains. Although the external appearance of the YE 2-6-0s was similar to the North British 2-6-0s still running on the line, the Yorkshire Engine Co. was involved in considerable redesign to bring the locomotives up to 1950s standards. Plate thickness and stays were improved to cope with a higher boiler pressure of 200lb psi. A welded steel firebox was produced by Jack Hadfield, Yorkshire Engine Co.'s number one welder, and modern valve gear introduced. A self-cleaning hopper-type ash pan was provided with high-pressure drenching. The boiler was pitched 6in higher to provide for the modifications and the leading truck brought forward 6in in order to bring the cylinders forward and to provide for a larger smoke box.[17] When the time came for the final inspection by the customer's inspector, the locomotive was fired up with coal. The inspector, however, insisted the locomotive should be fired up again with wood, the fuel to be used in Paraguay. Many duckboards from around the works disappeared to fuel the locomotive.[18]

A New York journalist described a trip behind one of the 2-6-0s in 1988:

> Rattling through Paraguay's rural interior on the Ferrocarril Presidente Carlos Antonio Lopez, I was dogged by the pungent aroma of burning wood… I was aboard the grand sounding El Internacional, which in reality was just a string of spartan second-class steel coaches trailing an old wooden dining car. We were chuffing our way towards Asuncion, Paraguay's capital, some 100 miles ahead. Up front plodding gamely was No.151, a wood burning steam locomotive built in England in 1953 by Yorkshire Engine Company.[19]

Such a journey is not possible today, but the two locomotives, No.151 Encarnacion and No.152 Asuncion (YE2513–2514) still survive in the Sapucai workshops in Paraguay. No.151 is said to be steamed occasionally for visitors.[20]

Two years later the Yorkshire Engine Co. despatched two 2-8-2s to the metre-gauge Chilean Northern following an order received in May 1952. Designed by the Yorkshire Engine Co. to a specification laid

YE2513 Encarnacion was delivered to Paraguay in 1953 with its sister locomotive YE2514 Asuncion. The Inspector would not approve the locomotive for delivery until he had seen it fired with wood. (Jean Rose Collection)

This photograph shows 151 of Central Paraguay Railway (YE2513) at the workshops of the railway in January 2007; both this locomotive and YE2514 survive and 151 is said to be steamed occasionally for visitors. (D. Welsby)

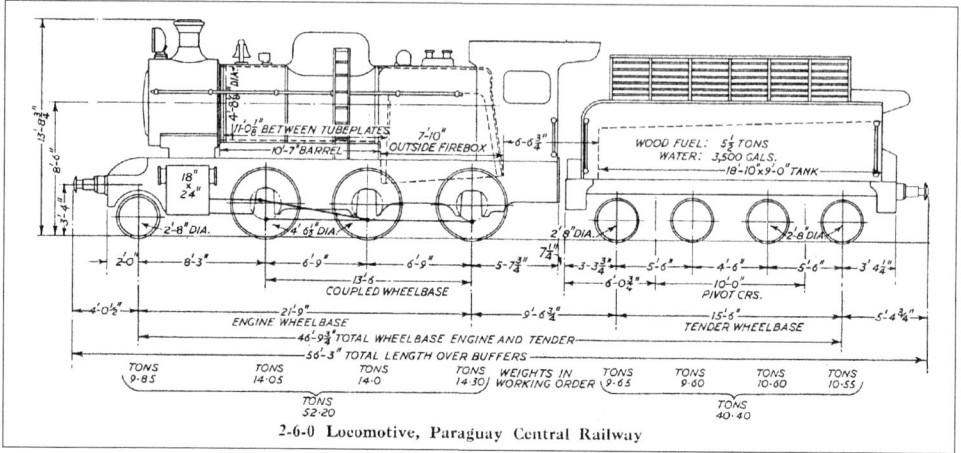

Drawing showing main dimensions of the Paraguay Central 2-4-0s YE2513–4. (Locomotive, December 1953)

down by consulting engineers Livesey & Henderson, the oil-burning locomotives (YE2554–5) were intended for mixed traffic. As with the locomotives for Paraguay, these two engines were a development of an earlier design. The three similar locomotives built in 1928 had a boiler pressure of 150lb psi and a tractive effort at 85 per cent boiler pressure of 25,050lb for an adhesive weight of 44 tons. The working pressure on the new locomotives was increased to 160lb psi and the tractive effort improved to 26,780lb for an adhesive weight of 46 tons. The extra weight was achieved by thickening the bar frames, stretchers and boiler plates and by the addition of ballast at the rear end to improve weight distribution.[21] The bar frames were about 4in thick and, during construction, cracks were found in the steel, which had to be replaced at the steel manufacturer's expense.

Steam locomotive overhauls, repairs and spares continued to be important business in the 1950s. As well as locomotives from United Steel branches, repairs were undertaken for the NCB collieries in the area and for the local Sheffield power station at Blackburn Meadows. Local steel and other works sending in locomotives included Goldendale Iron, Hepworth Iron, Hadfields and General Refractories. From further away, Darwen & Mostyn sent a Hunslet locomotive for overhaul and Bairds & Scottish Steel an elderly 0-6-0. This locomotive had been built at Stratford in 1890. It became LNER No.7690 and was first rebuilt in 1926. In 1952 it was again refurbished by the Yorkshire Engine Co. The work included re-boring the cylinders, new tyres and the addition of a sight feed lubricator and repainting. 'Painted black and lined, with a polished brass dome, the engine and tender presented an exceedingly smart appearance.'[22] Spares continued to be provided to the Indian Railways and to lines in Malaya, South America, Australia and Africa. Parts were supplied to other locomotive builders including Hunslet, North British, Vulcan Foundry and Hudswell Clarke. General engineering work for mainly local firms continued to occupy much of the time of the machine shop. It is said that the Yorkshire Engine Co. produced steel plates for the base of the reactor for the first nuclear power station at Calder Hall in the early 1950s.

Whilst continuing to manufacture steam locomotives, the Yorkshire Engine Co. commenced production of diesel electric locomotives. By initially choosing to build diesel electrics rather than diesel hydraulics, the requirement for new machinery was minimised. In contrast to steam locomotive production, the manufacture of diesel locomotives necessitated the company buying a significant proportion of each locomotive from outside suppliers. The Yorkshire Engine Co.'s most important collaborator was British Thomson Houston (BTH). BTH had been part of Associated Electrical Industries (AEI) since 1928. In 1960 the BTH name was dropped in favour of AEI, but in practice the Yorkshire Engine Co.'s supplier was unchanged. BTH provided the electrics for all Yorkshire Engine Co.'s diesels, irrespective of the engine manufacturer used. BTH engineers were often at the works ensuring the electrics were properly installed

No.915 (YE2554) is the first of two metre-gauge 2-8-2s built for the Chilean Northern Railway in 1955. (Jean Rose Collection)

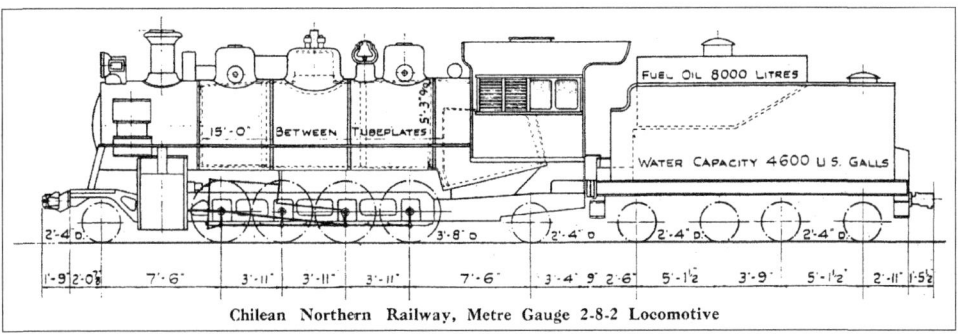

Drawing of Chilean Northern 2-8-2 (YE 2554–5). (Locomotive, February 1955)

and testing locomotives before despatch. On such days the works could be filled with a blue haze of smoke. Diesel locomotives did not always provide a cleaner environment for the workforce.

The first two 0-4-0 diesel electrics were built for Steel Peech & Tozer (YE2480–1) and used engines purchased from Davey Paxman, who would supply engines for all the early Yorkshire Engine Co. diesels. The engines were a modified version of a twelve-cylinder engine originally designed for marine use. Electrical equipment including generator and traction motors was provided by BTH. The locomotives were designed to meet the specific needs of steelworks. The cabs had to clear the casting stage, a structure within the melting shop, and the height was not to exceed 10ft 5in. The wheel base did not exceed 8ft to cope with the 70ft radius of the track in the melting shop.[23] The first locomotive was completed on 15 December 1950 and the second on 26 February 1951. The first was used for demonstration purposes for a few weeks and delivered after the second locomotive. As a consequence the first locomotive became No.2 *Rotherham* and the second No.1 *Sheffield*. Both have been preserved. No.1 is in the Kelham Island Industrial Museum in Sheffield and No.2 at Peak Rail near Matlock. Both are in poor condition, but the Kelham Island Museum plans to arrange a cosmetic restoration for No.1 as soon as funds become available.

Built in Stratford in 1890 and formerly LNER No.7690, this locomotive was completely overhauled and repainted by the Yorkshire Engine Co. in spring of 1952 for Bairds & Scottish Steel. (Jack Christmas Collection)

It might seem obvious today that the diesel locomotive would quickly replace steam in industrial applications, but this was not so clear at the time. The advantages of greater availability with a diesel had to be balanced against high initial costs and an anticipated high level of maintenance costs. When preparing its catalogue for industrial locomotives in 1952, the Yorkshire Engine Co. gave first place to its range of four standard steam locomotives. However, in terms of space both steam and diesel locomotives were given equal treatment and three pages were used to describe the merits of diesel. The advantage of the high tractive effort of a diesel at low speed was emphasised, plus fuel saving and the potential reduction in the number of locomotives required. Possible manpower savings were also outlined, as well as the absence of smoke. One factor which was to drive the change to diesel was the Clean Air Act of 1956 and the decision of British Railways to move to an all diesel fleet. Many overseas railways which might have been content to continue with steam were influenced by the decision of British Railways. As a consequence the market for steam locomotives overseas fell away.

The new Yorkshire Engine Co. catalogue of September 1952 introduced a range of four standard diesel electric locomotives. Designed principally for use in steelworks, customers were offered three 0-4-0 models designated DE1, DE2 and DE3 and one 0-6-0 designated DE4. The DE1 had a 'straight six' diesel engine of 240hp (Paxman R6PHL) and the DE2 a V6 of 275hp (Paxman V6RPHL II). The DE3 and DE4 were both to use the 400hp Paxman 12RPHL II engine. In practice the DE3 and DE4 were identical locomotives in terms of tractive effort. All those with 0-4-0 wheel configurations had 3ft 6in wheels and the 0-6-0s 3ft 8in wheels. The maximum tractive effort varied from 22,500lb in the DE1 to 30,000 in the DE3 and DE4. Only the DE2 was pictured in the catalogue by using one of the Steel Peech & Tozer 0-4-0s, even though its engine was only 240hp.[24]

Following delivery of the first two diesels to Steel Peech & Tozer in early 1951, a stock order was placed for another six 0-4-0DEs on 5 April 1951. Four sets of equipment were to be ordered immediately from BTH, with more later on Compton's instructions. It seems no orders were placed for engines, as these could vary depending on the power selected by the customer. Orders were, it would appear, expected from Steel Peech & Tozer and from Round Oak steel works, as Compton gave permission for parts which were standard for these two works to be ordered immediately. None of these locomotives were to be delivered for nearly two years.

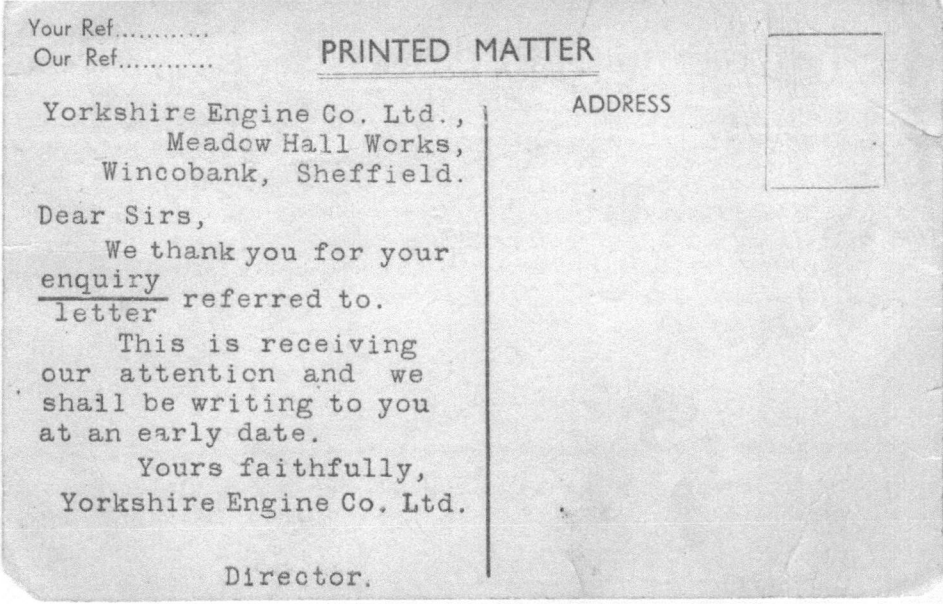

Acknowledgement postcard for enquiries showing a Chilean Northern 2-8-2 and a DE4 of the type supplied to Samuel Fox, John Summers and the NCB. (D. Harding Collection)

The last Type V 0-4-0STs (YE2585) were delivered to the Workington operations of United Steel in 1955. This is YE2585 under test prior to despatch to Workington Harbour & Dock Board. (Jean Rose Collection)

The largest customers in the early years of diesel production were not United Steel branches, which seem to have wanted to wait to see how the locomotives in the Templeborough melting shop at Steel, Peech & Tozer performed before ordering. A report in the *Locomotive* of June 1952 concerning the prototype 0-4-0s was to state they had 'given very satisfactory service'. A total of twenty-three DEs were delivered between March 1953 and December 1955, of which only six went to United Steel branches. The two largest customers were Lancashire Steel at Irlam who took eight 275hp DE2s and Stewarts & Lloyds who acquired five 275hp DE2s.

The Stewarts & Lloyds 275hp DE2s were delivered between March 1953 and January 1954 (YE2505–2509). They had been ordered in January 1952 with low height centre buffers, the normal side buffers over-riding the ingot bogies they were intended to pull, and were designed to cope with 90ft-radius curves. The original cab design had already been modified and this process of regular modification was to continue. The first locomotive, which was named *28 Coronation* to mark the Queen's Coronation in June 1953, experienced hot axle boxes on route to the works at Bilston and had to return to Meadowhall for modification. The subsequent four were called *29 Elizabeth*, *30 Phillip*, *31 Charles* and *32 Anne Elizabeth*. Before delivery to Stewarts & Lloyds, *Charles* had been on loan to ICI at Winnington as a demonstrator. ICI Winnington was to place a significant order in 1956.

During 1954–5 the first Yorkshire Engine Co. diesels were delivered to United Steel branches Samuel Fox and Distington Engineering, as well as two more to Steel Peech & Tozer. In addition John Summers' Hawarden steelworks in Cheshire, Round Oak steelworks and the NCB also purchased. The majority of the sales were 275hp DE2 0-4-0s, but four 400hp DE4s were also delivered. During its first five years of diesel production the Yorkshire Engine Co. had achieved a bigger spread of orders and customers for its diesel electrics than it had achieved for its industrial steam locomotives in the previous five years.

The 400hp 0-6-0 DE4 had, like the 275hp model, a Paxman engine. Its speed at continuous rating was 10mph. The wheel base was 11ft and the minimum rail clearance 7in. Carrying 400 gallons of fuel in

Stewarts & Lloyds No.32 Anne Elizabeth, a DE2 275hp 0-4-0 (YE2509), one of five delivered in 1952–3 to the Bilston works. (Jean Rose Collection)

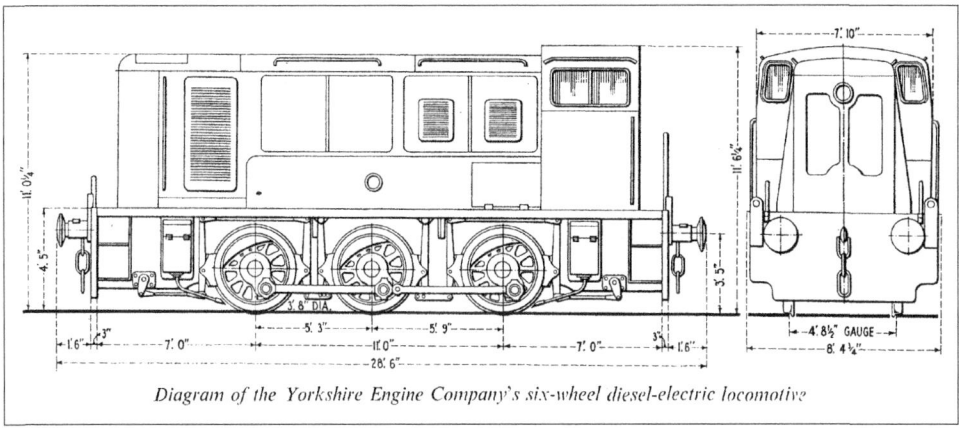

Drawing of DE4; two of these 400hp 0-6-0s were delivered to Samuel Fox in 1954, although the first DE4 had been delivered to John Summers' plant in Cheshire for use around the blast furnaces in 1953. (Diesel Railway Traction, March 1954)

two tanks, it weighed 51 tons. The DE4s went to John Summers, the East Midland Division of the NCB and Samuel Fox, which took two. Writing in *Fox News* in the autumn of 1956, the Traffic Manager for Samuel Fox, G.D. Illingworth, said the new 400hp locomotive has 'given rise to much interest and many questions'. In the article Illingworth debates whether Samuel Fox will go over entirely to diesel. He points out that the cost of the 400hp diesel is about £24,000 as against an equivalent 'steamer' at about £12,000. He expects the new locomotive to save fuel, have increased availability and be cheaper to maintain than an equivalent 'steamer'. He also comments on the removal of the smoke nuisance and expects reduced wear and tear on the track and rolling stock. He declines to make a final judgement on the suitability of the locomotive 'until our drivers are thoroughly used to it' and the financial impact can be assessed.

Diesel Railway Traction carried an advertisement for Yorkshire Engine Diesel Locomotives in August 1954 using the 400hp DE4 0-6-0 as an illustration. (Diesel Railway Traction)

Whilst Samuel Fox and others were assessing the quality of Yorkshire Engine Co.'s first diesel electrics, Technical Director Compton was developing a more radical 400hp 0-6-0 design, which was to be critical to the future of the business. It would be launched in 1956 and would, in effect, replace the DE4, of which only two more were made. Compton was now working with a new General Manager, E.R.S. Watkin, who had been appointed by United Steel on 1 September 1955.[25] Watkin was charged with bringing the business into profit. In the year to September 1955 the Yorkshire Engine Co. had made a loss of £129,536. By the end of the following year accumulated losses amounted to £372,912, which were covered by borrowings from the parent company. United Steel needed to see some return from its investment.

Notes

1. Interview with Mr Jack Christmas in March 2007; Jack Christmas joined the Yorkshire Engine Co. from school in 1936. He only managed to secure a job in the machine shop at Meadowhall because a friend's sister worked there. He volunteered for military service, but was never called up.
2. Interview with Mr Jack Christmas.
3. *SLS Journal* Volume 17 1946, p.239, lists the locomotives and the dimensions of their wheels and cylinders.
4. *History of United Steel Companies 1918–1968* by R. Peddie, p.50, and United Steel Finance Committee, 21 February 1945.
5. United Steel Managing Director's Advisory Committee (MDAC) minutes, 9 October 1946, which referred to a United Steel board of July 1946. The expenditure was already in hand.
6. Institution of Mechanical Engineers' and Institution of Locomotive Engineers' records.
7. Derek Penney and Peter Hawkins, former Yorkshire Engine employees.
8. Interviews with Mr R.W. Bassendale and Mr Jack Christmas.
9. MDAC, September 1946.
10. MDAC, May 1947.
11. 2483–2489 were made to stock as Type I and allocated as requested by Unites Steel subsidiaries.
12. Industrial Railway Record, pp.2–16, February 1969, by H.A. Gamble, who quotes from Hunslet regarding the YE locomotives: 'They could have been built to "Austerity" drawings but we have no confirmation on this point.'
13. *Railway World*, July 1987, p.415, 'Hunslet's Steam Production 1949–971' by Don Townsley.
14. Letters from Mrs Vera Brown, March 2007.
15. *Railway World*, May 1987, p.281, 'Hunslet's Steam Production' 1949–1971 by Don Townsley.
16. Peter Hawkins.
17. *Locomotive*, December 1953, p.196–7, July 1910, p.137; *Locomotive International No 65; Railway Gazette*, November 1953, pp.521–2.
18. Interview with Derek Penney, retired Yorkshire Engine Co. draughtsman.
19. 'By Wood Burner from Buenos Ayres', *New York Times*, 19 May 2006.
20. Email from Darrien Welsby, 7 July 2007.
21. *Railway Gazette*, January 1955, pp.45–46; *Locomotive*, February 1955, pp.16–17.
22. *Locomotive*, June 1952, p.99.
23. *Locomotive*, March 1951, p.36.
24. *Diesel Railway Traction*, December 1953, p.266.
25. United Steel, MDAC 5.

7

The Final Years
1956–1965

YE built a total of 377 diesel locomotives between 1951 and 1965. Sales of diesel locomotives rose markedly in 1956. Between 1958 and 1961 output every year exceeded forty locomotives, with the best year being 1960 when over fifty locomotives were completed. Sales of locomotives may not, however, directly match revenue, since individual locomotives could cost as little as £9,000 or as much as £30,000. The business was profitable from the year to September 1957 to the year to September 1963. Much of the accumulated losses of the early 1950s were clawed back, but, by the time the decision was taken to close, the business was again losing money and the UK market for industrial diesels was shrinking. The prospect of locomotive sales overseas and the general engineering business still undertaken in the machine shop and forge was insufficient to justify keeping the plant open.

Of the 377 diesel locomotives built, 102 were of a single basic design. Launched to the press at United Steel's Appleby Frodingham branch in Scunthorpe on 19 April 1956, the 0-6-0 400hp Janus locomotive was probably the Yorkshire Engine Co.'s most successful and adventurous design. Compton had travelled to the United States and seen diesel electric locomotives with twin engines and a central cab. He concluded this style could meet the requirements of many UK industrial clients as well as the needs of United Steel's own businesses. Named Janus after the Roman god who is typically depicted with two faces, the design created considerable interest. The main departure from usual British practice was the division of the power unit into two identical packs. Each pack of engine, radiator and generator powered a traction motor on the respective outer axle. This arrangement left the central cab free from the underfloor transmission seen in other designs and improved the driver's outlook, since each bonnet contained only a single high-speed 200hp engine. With one generator connected to a single traction motor the power control system was simplified and maintenance made easier. The cost of twin high-speed power units was no greater than the cost of a single 400hp low-speed unit. An important new feature, which was subsequently copied by other manufacturers, was the provision of step-in or recessed platforms for the shunter at both ends of the locomotive.[1]

The first Janus (YE2594) had been delivered to Appleby Frodingham on 2 March 1956, so the works had seven weeks for the drivers to get acquainted with the new locomotive before the press and customer launch on 19 April. The guests, who had been put up in hotels around Scunthorpe on the previous night, assembled at the works at 10.30 a.m. for a series of talks and demonstrations. The Janus brought 375 tons of ore from the workings to the blast furnaces up gradients of 1:70 to 1:50. It shunted ingot cars from the melting shop to the stripping shed and transferred the slag ladles from the furnaces to the tip. All the United Steel branches were represented as well as potential customers including the Crown Agents, the British Transport Commission, the National Coal Board and Lysaghts, the other Scunthorpe steelmaker. There were eighteen members of the press present from local papers in the Sheffield area and from the railway and engineering journals. Rolls-Royce, who provided the engines, and BTH, who made the electrics, sent representatives. Watkin and Compton presided. *Engineering* reported in June 1956:

YE2594 was the first Janus delivered to Appleby Frodingham and used at the press launch in 1956. It was still in operation over fifty years later at Corus Stocksbridge, once a United Steel branch. YE2594 is entering the Ellencliffe loop at Deepcar on 21 September 2006. (Andrew Hurrell)

A Rolls-Royce-powered Janus being delivered to United Steel's Appleby Frodingham branch by Jack Christmas. (Jack Christmas Collection)

A joint advertisement between Rolls-Royce and Yorkshire Engine Co. of 1958 promotes the 400hp Janus. The Yorkshire Grey symbol is used but without the usual line 'A good pull from the start'.

Very high performance has been obtained with this locomotive at Scunthorpe, but this is necessary as even with a seventeen-year-old steam locomotive an availability of 74 per cent was usual. The diesel has been working for continuous periods of nine days, 24 hours a day, at the end of which time it has been taken to the shops for a check-over. This has taken only seven hours as against the 24 required for a steam engine.[2]

The Janus weighed 48 tons in working order. The tractive effort at the start was 30,000lb and at a continuous speed of 8mph was 13,100lb. The maximum permissible speed was 23mph. The 3ft 8in coupled wheels were 5ft 6in apart between centres. Roller bearings were used to reduce the necessity for lubrication. The 400hp locomotive used two Rolls-Royce C6SFL engines. A 200hp 'half Janus' was also produced as either a 0-4-0 or 0-6-0. It shared the same general design and engine but was not demonstrated on the day. The first 'half Janus' 0-6-0 (YE2603) had been delivered to United Steel's Distington Engineering branch in Cumbria on 6 October 1955 and a second (YE2604) to Brymbo Steelworks, not a United Steel business, on 16 January 1956. The first 'half Janus' was found to be too light and extra weight was added by making the frame thicker.

The first major customer to acquire a fleet of Janus was the Port of London Authority for its Tilbury docks complex. Ten 400hp Janus were delivered between November 1956 and June 1959, later examples going to the Royal Docks. The Port of London Authority was to be one of the Yorkshire Engine Co.'s

The first Rolls-Royce 200hp 0-4-0 diesel electric (YE2603), sometimes called a 'half Janus', was delivered to Distington Engineering, a United Steel branch, in October 1955. (Derek Penney Collection)

A 500hp Cummins-engined Janus awaiting despatch at Meadowhall; five Cummins-engined diesels were delivered to Appleby Frodingham in 1963–4 at a price of £24,960 each. (Derek Penney Collection)

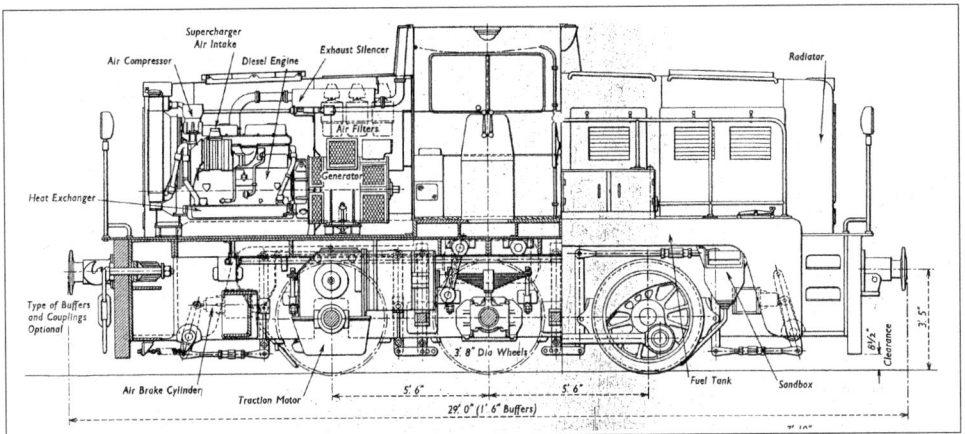

Engineering ran a product profile on the Janus in December 1961 incorporating both a drawing of a Janus and a chart showing how the Port of London Authority had reduced costs following the change from steam to diesel. (Engineering, 22 December 1961)

largest customers outside the United Steel Group and purchased a total of twenty-seven locomotives by the end of June 1961. As a result of the success of the early Janus, the Authority placed an order for a further £350,000 of locomotives in July 1958.[3] It also acquired six 220hp 0-4-0 diesel electrics for the India and Millwall docks and eleven 300hp 0-6-0 diesel electrics. The 220hp 0-4-0s used the Janus engine, which had by then been up-rated by 10 per cent. Janus locomotives with Rolls-Royce engines delivered after January 1960 were, therefore, 440hp as opposed to the original 400hp. The Port of London Authority's 300hp 0-6-0s used the Rolls-Royce C8S engine, with a maximum tractive effort of 26,000lb and a top speed of 22mph. The 220hp 0-4-0, now with a tractive effort of 19,000lb and a top speed of 20mph, weighed 30 tons. The 300hp 0-6-0 weighed 40 tons.[4]

Figures supplied to *Engineering* in December showed that the Port of London Authority's fuel and maintenance costs had dropped substantially as a result of the change from steam to diesel. It was generally accepted at the time that fuel costs would drop by 75 per cent when switching from steam to diesel. By taking a range of locomotives from the Yorkshire Engine Co., spares could be standardised. The ten Janus and the six 220hp locomotives had the same engines. Many of the parts of the 300hp engine were the same as those used in the 220hp engine. The Port of London Authority told *Engineering*: 'All these locomotives have given every satisfaction and the overhaul life of 9,000 engine hours quoted by Rolls-Royce offers every prospect of being handsomely exceeded.'[5] The Port of London Authority closed all its railways in 1970 and the Yorkshire Engine Co. fleet was sold to other industrial operators. A number survive today in industrial use and on preserved lines.

Apart from the Port of London Authority, only one large industrial company outside the United Steel group took a significant number of Janus locomotives. ICI (Imperial Chemical Industries) took twelve 400hp Janus between December 1957 and March 1959 for their major chemical plant at Billingham. The order was worth £300,000 and replaced a fleet of eighteen steam locomotives;[6] the new locomotives were named after local dales 'Allendale', 'Farndale' and 'Bilsdale' for example (YE2629, 2665-6, 2714, 2718-9, 2723-5, 2741-3). To encourage the purchase ICI had had the use of a demonstrator for some months in 1957. ICI had already purchased five 0-4-0 diesel electrics with 235hp engines (YE2609-2613) for use at their Lostock, Winnington and Wallerscote works, where the company was also using diesels supplied by English Electric and Ruston & Hornsby. ICI subsequently purchased five 220hp 0-4-0 diesel hydraulics for its Runcorn operations.

In spite of good press reports and the wide use of the Janus in United Steel plants, the Yorkshire Engine Co. must have been disappointed that comparatively few Janus were sold to steelworks outside the United Steel group. Brymbo steelworks took two, Shelton Iron & Steel three and Stanton Iron one. Two metre-gauge versions went to the Indian Fertilizer Corporation and one standard gauge to the Aluminium Union in Jamaica. Apart from the NCB, which took five, the rest of the sales were to United Steel branches. An attempt to sell to British Railways by lending the Eastern Region a Janus in the summer of 1956 was unsuccessful. Many Janus, however, survive and are still used in steelworks in the Sheffield and Scunthorpe areas, a tribute to the robust design. This is the Janus used for the demonstration at Appleby Frodingham in April 1956 and is still operational at Stocksbridge, near Sheffield in 2008, more than fifty years after construction.

Most Janus were built using two Rolls-Royce C6S engines of 200hp or, after 1960, the up-rated 220hp version of the engine. However, by 1962 the Yorkshire Engine Co. had become increasingly concerned that Rolls-Royce was a potential threat to its business. Rolls-Royce had acquired Sentinel in 1956 and reorganised the works at Shrewsbury to build diesel locomotives in competition with the Yorkshire Engine Co. and other independent locomotive manufacturers using Rolls-Royce engines. The Yorkshire Engine Co. therefore decided to offer customers for Janus and other locomotives a choice of Cummins or Rolls-Royce Engines. The Cummins engines were rated at 250hp and seven Janus supplied to Appleby Frodingham had Cummins engines and were rated 500hp in total. The price to the customer was the same. A Janus supplied to Appleby Frodingham in 1963-4 cost about £25,000 irrespective of the engine used. The Indian Fertilizer Corporation paid £26,500 each for its two metre-gauge locomotives.

PURCHASERS OF JANUS LOCOMOTIVES

Customer	Nos Acquired	Delivery Dates
Appleby Frodingham (United Steel Branch)	42	1956–65
Aluminium Union Port Esquival Jamaica	1	1959
Brymbo Steel Works	2	1962
ICI Billingham	12	1957–59
Indian Fertilizer Corporation Assam	2	1963
NCB Various Divisions	6	1958–59
Port of London Authority	10	1956–59
Samuel Fox (United Steel Branch)	8	1957–59
Steel Peech & Tozer (United Steel Branch)	4	1964–65
Shelton Iron & Steel	3	1960 & 1962
Stanton Iron	1	1958
United Coke & Chemicals (United Steel Branch)	3	1959–62
United Steel Ore Mining (United Steel Branch)	8	1959–63
Total	102	

Sixty-five of the 102 Janus locomotives were acquired by United Steel branches. At least thirty have survived to 2008. About seventeen of the thirty-four are still in regular or occasional use around the steelworks at Scunthorpe in Lincolnshire (formerly Appleby Frodingham), at Stocksbridge near Sheffield (formerly Samuel Fox) and at Aldwarke, Rotherham, which was not a United Steel branch. Figures for operational locomotives are imprecise, since some are kept for spares. Most of the operational locomotives have undergone significant modification over the last fifty years. None now use Cummins engines. Some

Only two 0-6-0 DE2s with the 275hp Paxman engine were built; YE2617 and YE2618 were delivered to North West Gas in May 1958. (Derek Penney Collection)

have been adapted for radio control, had turbocharged engines installed or been fitted with air brakes and noise reduction measures. A few Janus survive on preserved railways.

By the late 1950s the Yorkshire Engine Co. realised that it needed to be able to offer diesel hydraulic as well as diesel electric locomotives. In December 1958 the Yorkshire Engine Co. announced the introduction of two versions of a 170hp diesel hydraulic locomotive for light industrial use. 0-4-0 and 0-6-0 models were available and were fitted with the C6N version of the Rolls-Royce engine used in the Janus and 'half Janus'. The engine was set in the frame at an inclination of 13 degrees to the horizontal so that the torque converter output shaft drove directly through the axle-hung double-reduction gear box below the cab floor. The Rolls-Royce engines were built at Shrewsbury and the torque converter at Crewe. The introduction of these locomotives widened the market for Yorkshire Engine Co. locomotives and offered a price reduction to the customer. A diesel hydraulic typically cost around 10 per cent less than a diesel electric locomotive of similar capacity.[7]

By the early 1960s the Yorkshire Engine Co. had extended its range of models using Rolls-Royce and other engines. The range included both diesel hydraulic and diesel electric 0-4-0s and 0-6-0s using both the Rolls-Royce C6 and C8 engines in their various forms. It had also developed two 600hp 0-8-0s diesel hydraulics with central cabs on similar lines to the Janus. Taurus was designed for use by main line railways and Indus for industrial customers, but neither found a significant market. The DE2 with a 275hp Davy Paxman engine continued to be offered to customers and was the last locomotive allocated a works number (YE2953). The 400hp DE4 had effectively been replaced by the Janus. To provide a better choice to customers and to avoid too great a dependence on Rolls-Royce, customers were offered the choice of Cummins or Rolls-Royce engines for Janus and some other models. The Yorkshire Engine Co. was willing to vary the design of each locomotive to meet specific customer needs. From 1960 onwards the electrical equipment carried the AEI label following the renaming of BTH.

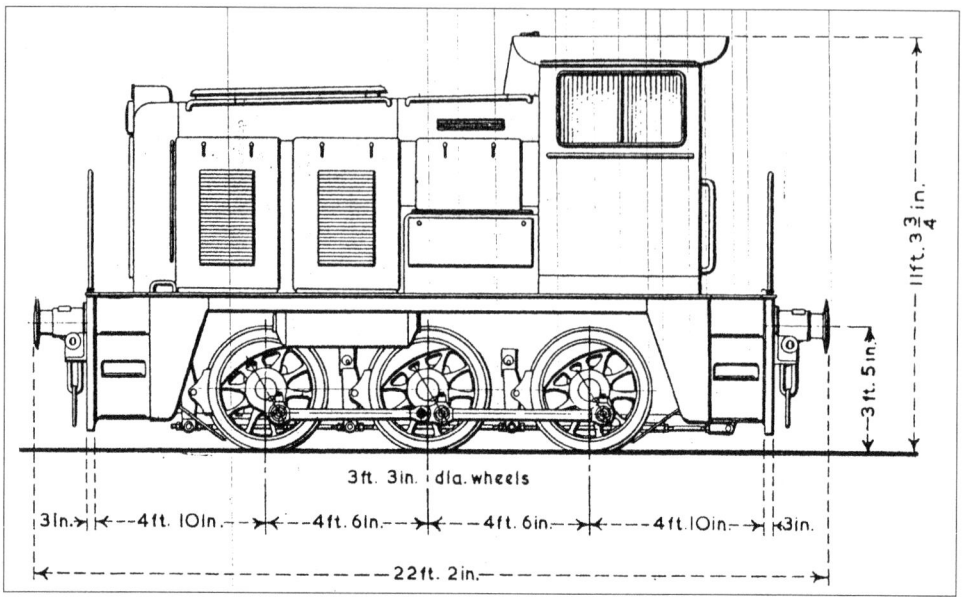

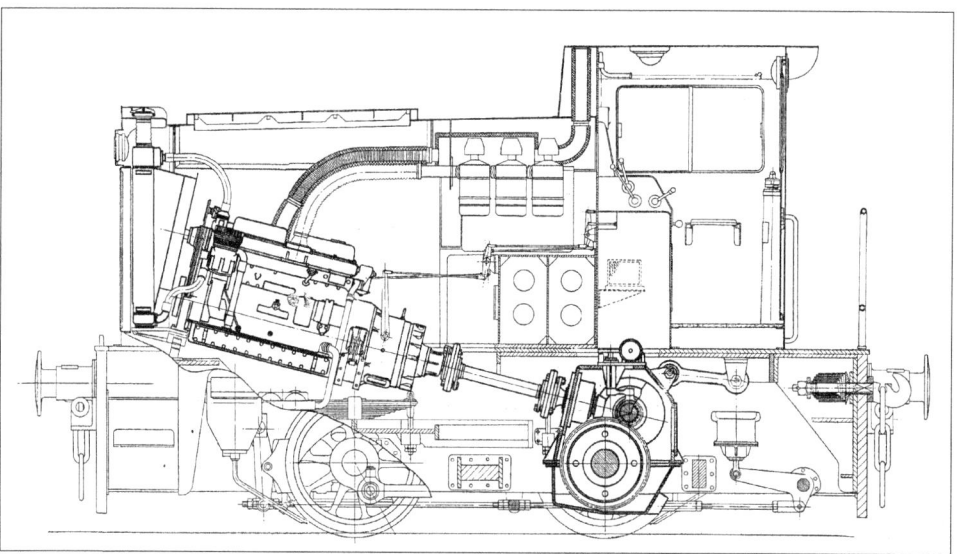

The Yorkshire Engine Co. needed to offer diesel hydraulic as well as diesel electric locomotives if its range was to remain competitive. The introduction of its 0-4-0 and 0-6-0 DH 170hp DH range was announced to the press in December 1958. (Railway Gazette and Yorkshire Engine Co. Spec)

YORKSHIRE ENGINE LOCOMOTIVES powered by Rolls-Royce Engines[8]

Power	Wheel Arrangement	Typical Weight In Tons	Maximum Tractive Effort	Maximum Speed	Engine Type
Diesel Electric					
220	0-4-0	30	19000	20	C6S
220	0-6-0	30	19000	20	C6S
300	0-4-0	40	26000	22	C8S
300	0-6-0	40	26000	22	C8S
440 Janus	0-6-0	48	34000	23	2 X C6S
Diesel Hydraulic					
170	0-4-0	28	16400	18	C6N
170	0-6-0	30	18800	16	C6N
220	0-4-0	30	19200	20	C6S
220	0-6-0	32	22000	18	C6S
300	0-4-0	40	27000	19	C8S
300	0-6-0	60	27000	19	C8S
600 Taurus	0-8-0	60	45000	34	2 X C8S
600 Indus	0-8-0	60	46000	22	2 X C8S

The first 170hp diesel hydraulic was supplied to the Central Electricity Generating Board (CEGB) Yorkshire Division (YE2673) on 26 August 1959, some eight months after the press coverage. The CEGB were subsequently to return with an order for three 300hp 0-6-0 diesel hydraulics for Skelton Grange in 1961 (YE2835–2837). The first 220hp diesel hydraulic went to Staveley Iron & Chemical in December 1959 (YE2676). The first substantial order for five 220hp 0-4-0 diesel hydraulics came from ICI's Castner-Kellner works at Runcorn for delivery in July and August 1960 (YE2804–2808). When first delivered, these locomotives had problems with their brakes. The special non-sparking Ferrodo brake lining wore out quickly and modifications had to be made.[9] The locomotives were designed to work in tandem and numbered CK1-5.

Most steelworks purchased diesel electric rather than diesel hydraulic locomotives from the Yorkshire Engine Co. The exception was RTB (Richard, Thomas & Baldwins) which had steelworks at Llanwern and Ebbw Vale. Six 300hp 0-4-0s diesel hydraulics were delivered to Ebbw Vale between February 1961 and March 1963 and numbered 120–125 (YE2822-4 and YE2840–2842). In the same period RTB's Spencer works at Llanwern took delivery of ten 300hp 0-6-0 diesel hydraulics numbered 1–10 (YE2825–2834) and a single 600hp 0-8-0 Indus. The 300hp DHs were fitted out for tandem operation. The Indus (YE2893) was one of only two Indus built and was delivered on 2 August 1962. The second Indus went in the same month to Stewarts & Lloyds (YE2894). *Modern Transport* commented on the Indus: 'These machines have the robust frame and well-balanced dimensions which are characteristic of Yorkshire Engine designs.'[10]

When the Stewarts & Lloyds' Indus was delivered, it came off the rails. Bernard Ledger, a senior fitter, and Jack Christmas, an inspector, were sent down to the works from the Yorkshire Engine Co. to sort out the problem. They found the springs were faulty and contacted Meadowhall to have the rest of the batch returned to the supplier. Subsequently the Indus was found to be much more efficient than the steam engine it had replaced. The drivers were earning such high bonuses under the piece-work system that they had to be transferred to a fixed salary.[11]

This 220hp 0-4-0 DH is probably YE2676, which was delivered to Staveley Iron & Chemicals in Derbyshire in 1959. The locomotive is now known as Tiny II and operates at Bombadier Transportation's Crewe works following a period at Cawoods, Cheltenham, from 1973–85. (Derek Penney Collection)

YE2661 Arnold Machin, a 200hp DE, was delivered to Eccles Slag at Scunthorpe in 1959. It is now owned by the Appleby Frodingham Railway Preservation Society and may be seen on one of the Society's regular steelworks tours. (Author)

YE2804 was the first of five 220hp 0-4-0 DHs delivered to the Castner Kellner works of ICI in July 1960. (Derek Penney Collection)

RTB was one of the Yorkshire Engine Co.'s main customers for diesel hydraulics. The photograph shows Jack Christmas, the Yorkshire Engine Co. Service Engineer, handing over YE2825, a 300hp 0-6-0 DH, to G. Morgan, RTB's Locomotive Maintenance Foreman at Llanwern, with Gordon Griffiths, Rail Traffic Foreman, standing by on 13 April 1961. The locomotive survives in 2008 at Corus Skinningrove, Saltburn. (Jack Christmas Collection)

YE2832 and 2831 (RTB Llanwern nos 8 and 7) are in operation in tandem at the plant. (Derek Penney Collection)

Two steelworks purchased a single 0-8-0 Indus each. The photograph shows YE2893 outside the Yorkshire Engine Co.'s office block, awaiting delivery to RTB Llanwern in August 1962. (Derek Penney Collection)

The second 600hp 0-8-0 DH Indus was delivered to Stewarts & Lloyds in August 1962; the photograph shows the locomotive at Pen Green in May 1965. (Alec Swain – Transport Treasury)

Piece work systems were in use at Meadowhall throughout the 1950s and 1960s. A team of two fitters and an apprentice would have responsibility for a locomotive. The team was paid on piecework with each aspect of the operation priced. For every new locomotive design a price had to be worked out for each operation. A good week's wages in the period was £16. Each locomotive took about six to ten weeks to build. Frames were rough cut from steel plate and one marked out for machining. Either two or three sets of frames were then bolted together and machined in one go. The team would be responsible for construction and testing of the locomotive with specialists such as electricians and drillers called in as required during the assembly work.[12]

Over 200 diesel locomotives were supplied to the iron and steel industry and related trades such as refractory brick manufacturing and slag processing, just under half being supplied to other branches of United Steel. Even if the Janus was not as popular as the Yorkshire Engine Co. might have hoped, the DE2 with a 275hp Davy Paxman engine sold well within the steel industry, as well as the 0-4-0 DEs with 200/220hp Rolls-Royce engines.

YORKSHIRE ENGINE UK DIESEL CUSTOMERS Iron, Steel and Related Industries

Customer	Locomotives – Type and Number Acquired	Total
Appleby Frodingham (United Steel branch)	Janus (42)	42
Barrow Steelworks (United Steel branch)	220hp 0-4-0 DE (2)	2
Brightside Foundry	170hp 0-4-0 DH (1)	1
Brymbo Steelworks	Janus (2), 200hp 0-6-0 DE (5)	7
Clugston Cawood	200hp 0-6-0 DE (1)	1

No.93 (YE2889) was one of six 300hp DEs delivered to Parkgate Iron & Steel in 1962–3. It continues in use at Corus Aldwarke in Rotherham in August 2007. (Andrew Hurrell)

Janus No.32 (YE2935), which was delivered to Steel Peech & Tozer in Rotherham in 1964, waits by the weighbridge at Corus's Aldwarke site in the summer of 2007. (Andrew Hurrell)

YE2793 was a 440hp Janus delivered to the United Steel ore mining branch in February 1961 and is still available for use at Corus Scunthorpe in 2008 carrying No.53. (Alec Swain – Transport Treasury)

Darwen & Mostyn Iron	200hp 0-4-0 DE (1), 220hp 0-4-0 DE (1)	2
Distington Engineering (United Steel branch)	200hp 0-6-0 DE (1)	1
Eccles Slag	200hp 0-6-0 DE (1)	1
John Summers	400hp DE4 (1)	1
Lancashire Steel	Irlam 275hp 0-4-0 DE2 (18), Warrington 200hp 0-4-0 DE (2)	20
Parkgate Iron & Steel	300hp 0-6-0 DE (6)	6
Round Oak	275hp 0-4-0 DE2 (10)	10
Richard Thomas & Baldwins (RTB)	300hp 0-6-0 DH (10), 300hp 0-4-0 DH (6), 800hp DH Indus (1)	17
Stewarts & Lloyds	275hp 0-4-0 DE2 (13), 800hp Indus 0-8-0 (1)	14
Samuel Fox (United Steel)	Janus (8), 275hp DE2 (1), 400hp DE4 (4)	13
Shelton Iron & Steel	Janus (3), 220hp 0-4-0 DE (4)	7
Steel, Peech & Tozer (United Steel)	Janus (4), 200hp 0-4-0 DE (3), 250hp DE (2), 275hp DE2 (10)	19
Stanton Iron	Janus (1), 200hp 0-4-0 DE (5), 275hp DE2 (5), 300hp DE (1)	12
Staveley Iron & Chemicals	220hp 0-4-0 DH	1
Steetley	Oughtibridge Silica 200hp 0-4-0 DE(1), Doloma 220hp 0-4-0 DE (1)	2
United Coke & Chemicals (United Steel)	Janus (3)	3
United Steel Ore Mining	Janus (8), 220 0-6-0 DE (3)	11

Whitehead Iron & Steel	200hp 0-4-0 DE	1
Workington Iron & Steel (United Steel)	200hp 0-4-0 DE (9), 220hp 0-4-0 DE (1), 275hp 0-4-0 DE2 (4), 300hp 0-4-0 DH (5)	19
Workington Harbour (United Steel)	200hp 0-4-0 DE (2)	2
	Total	215

Customers outside the coal and steel industries were much more important to the Yorkshire Engine Co. during the diesel years than they had been in steam days. The NCB continued to provide a fair level of orders for a diverse range of diesel locomotives and Meadowhall continued to receive general repair business from the coal mining industry. However, the major new UK customers were Imperial Chemical Industries and the Port of London Authority who bought over twenty locomotives each.

YORKSHIRE ENGINE UK DIESEL CUSTOMERS.
excluding Iron, Steel and related trades and British Railways

Customer	Locomotives Purchased	Number
AEI	220hp 0-4-0 DE (1)	1
Barnsley District Coking	200hp 0-4-0 DE (1)	1
Central Electricity Generating Board	300hp 0-6-0 DE (3), 170hp 0-4-0 DH (1)	4
Esso Trafford Park	200hp 0-4-0 DE (1)	1
Hutchinson Estate & Dock	170hp DH (1)	1
Imperial Chemical Industries	Janus (12), 235hp 0-4-0 DE (5), 220hp 0-4-0 DH (5)	22
National Coal Board	Janus (6), 200hp 0-6-0 DE (1), 220hp 0-6-0 DH (1), 220hp 0-6-0 DE (1), 220hp 0-4-0 DH (2), 300hp 0-6-0 DH (3), 375hp 0-6-0 DH (5), 400hp 0-6-0 DE4 (1)	20
North West Gas	275 0-6-0 DE (2)	2
Pilkington	170hp 0-4-0 DH (3), 200hp 0-4-0 DH (7)	10
Port of London Authority	Janus (10), 220 0-4-0 DE (6), 300hp 0-6-0 DE (11)	27
REA Limited	200hp 0-4-0 DE (1)	1
South Yorkshire Chemicals	220 0-4-0 DH (2)	2
	Total	92

Yorkshire Engine Co. made considerable efforts to win business from British Railways. As the last Western Region Pannier tanks were being built at Meadowhall in the summer of 1956, British Railways Eastern Region had the use of a Janus (YE2595) before it was delivered to Appleby Frodingham in August; no orders resulted. A year later the Yorkshire Engine Co. was appointed a subcontractor to BTH for a British Transport Commission order for ten Type 1 Class 15 locomotives D8200–8209 (YE2642–2651). Davey Paxman supplied the 800hp engines, BTH the electrics and Clayton Equipment the superstructure. The Yorkshire Engine Co. was responsible for the under-frame and the locomotives were erected at Meadowhall. Designed for local passenger and freight traffic, the first locomotive was delivered in November 1957 and was of sufficient interest for a Movietone news cameraman to record the proceedings. Unfortunately the locomotives were not known for their reliability and were withdrawn by 1971.[13]

The Yorkshire Engine Co. was more successful three years later when it secured an order from British Railways for twenty 170hp 0-4-0 diesel hydraulic shunters. These locomotives were very similar in design to the 170hp 0-4-0 DHs delivered to the Yorkshire Engine Co.'s industrial customers. They replaced elderly steam engines in docks and similar locations where the loading gauge was restricted and the

YE2679 is a 220hp DH supplied to South Yorkshire Chemicals in April 1962. It worked at Ford's Halewood factory from 1971 to 1996. Refurbished in 2006 at Long Marston, it is now at Peak Rail. (Peter Briddon)

YE2708 was one of six Janus purchased by the NCB. It was delivered to the NCB Northern Division in March 1959 and is shown at Ashington Colliery on 10 June 1967. (Alec Swain – Transport Treasury)

YE2749 was one of two 400hp Janus supplied to the NCB's North West Area 2 in September 1959. (Jack Christmas Collection)

The Port of London Authority was one of the Yorkshire Engine Co.'s best customers for diesel electrics. YE2756 was one of eleven 0-6-0 DEs supplied between September 1959 and January 1960. No.231 was the second locomotive delivered. (Derek Penney Collection)

Ten British Railways Class 15 locomotives were assembled by Yorkshire Engine at Meadowhall for BTH in 1957; this photograph shows one of the locomotives in the yard at Meadowhall awaiting inspection. (B.N. Collins – Howard Turner Collection)

curvature of the line tight. The first locomotive was delivered in October 1960 and the last in November 1961 (YE2809–2818 and YE2843–2852). Numbered D2850–2869, these locomotives formed British Rail Class 02. The typical Yorkshire Engine Co. design of a cab door at the rear and a railed platform behind the cab was unusual on British Railways. They were deployed initially in the Merseyside and Manchester areas and were well regarded for the duties they had to perform. As networks were slimmed and the need for their services on British Railways declined, most were withdrawn between 1969 and 1973 and sold on to industrial customers.[14] Seven still survive and are now used on preserved lines, including one for shunting duties at the National Railway Museum. A number of pseudo members of the class can be found on preserved railways, where some of the Yorkshire Engine Co.'s very similar ex-industrial 0-4-0s of 170hp and 220hp, DE and DH, have been dressed up as Class 02s with British Railways' livery and a false number.

As Meadowhall delivered the Class 02 170hp shunters to British Railways, the Yorkshire Engine Co. set about trying to secure orders for its 600hp 0-8-0 Taurus. The locomotive (YE2875) was given a trial on British Railways in the spring of 1961. It was designed to fill what was perceived by Yorkshire Engine to be a gap between the pure shunting engine of up to about 400hp and the 800–1,000hp Bo-Bo locomotive of the type assembled by the Yorkshire Engine Co. in 1957–8. The Taurus was described as 'A versatile locomotive of special interest to railways needing an economical unit for heavy shunting and transfer or trip working on main lines.'[15] With the central cab design of the Janus, the locomotive was powered by two Rolls-Royce C8SFL engines. The locomotives started away using only one engine. The second power unit came into play above speeds of about 3.5mph and, with both engines in use, a satisfactory speed of 35mph could be achieved for hauling trains of up to about 500 tons out on the line. Unfortunately British Railways did not buy and the locomotive appears to have been returned to Meadowhall and dismantled. Many of the components could be used in similar locomotives, most probably in a Taurus supplied to Spain in April 1963. The role the Taurus might have fulfilled for British Railways was largely undertaken by the BR Class 14 locomotives.

The Yorkshire Engine Co.'s sole major order for diesel locomotives for British Railways was for twenty 170hp 0-4-0 DHs in 1960–1. Known as Class 02 the photograph shows members of the team responsible probably with the last of the class. From left to right: Doug Jessop, Bernard Thorpe, -?-, Bernard Ogden, -?-, George Lawless, -?-, -?-, Joe Allan (Erecting Shop Foreman), -?-. Seated on engine: Donald Peacock and Allen Stocks. Standing on engine: Chas Howard. (Elsecar Steam Railway)

D2853 (YE2812) was in use for an Appleby Frodingham Preservation Society rail tour on 21 April 2007. Some seven of the Class 02s survive including one at the National Railway Museum. (Author)

YE2677 is a 170hp DH delivered to Pilkington in May 1960. Since 1999 it has been based at Ribble steam and painted as if it was a British Railways Class 02 D2870. The last British Railways 02 was numbered D2869. D2870 is a 'fictitious' number, but the locomotive is very similar to a Class 02. (Andrew Hurrell)

This 600hp 0-8-0 Diesel Hydraulic 'Taurus' (YE2875) was designed for use on main line railways and went on loan to British Railways in the spring of 1961. British Railways declined to buy. (Derek Penney Collection)

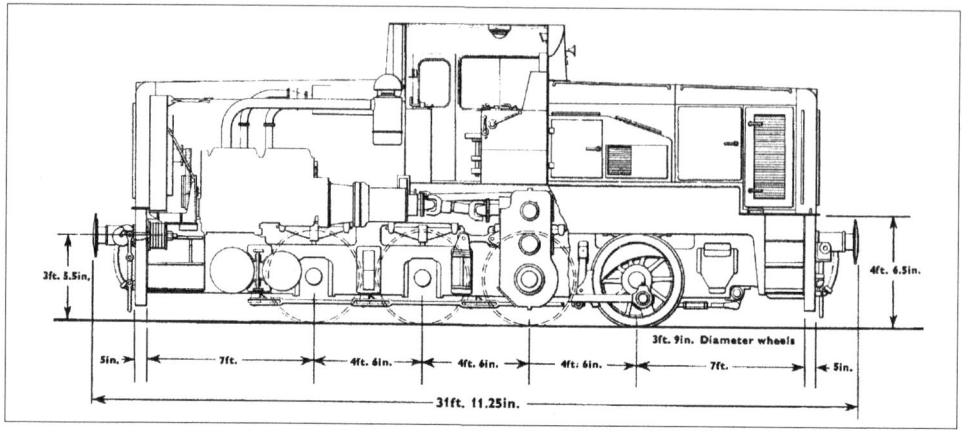

A drawing from a Rolls-Royce specification indicates the key features of the Taurus design. (Rolls-Royce Specification)

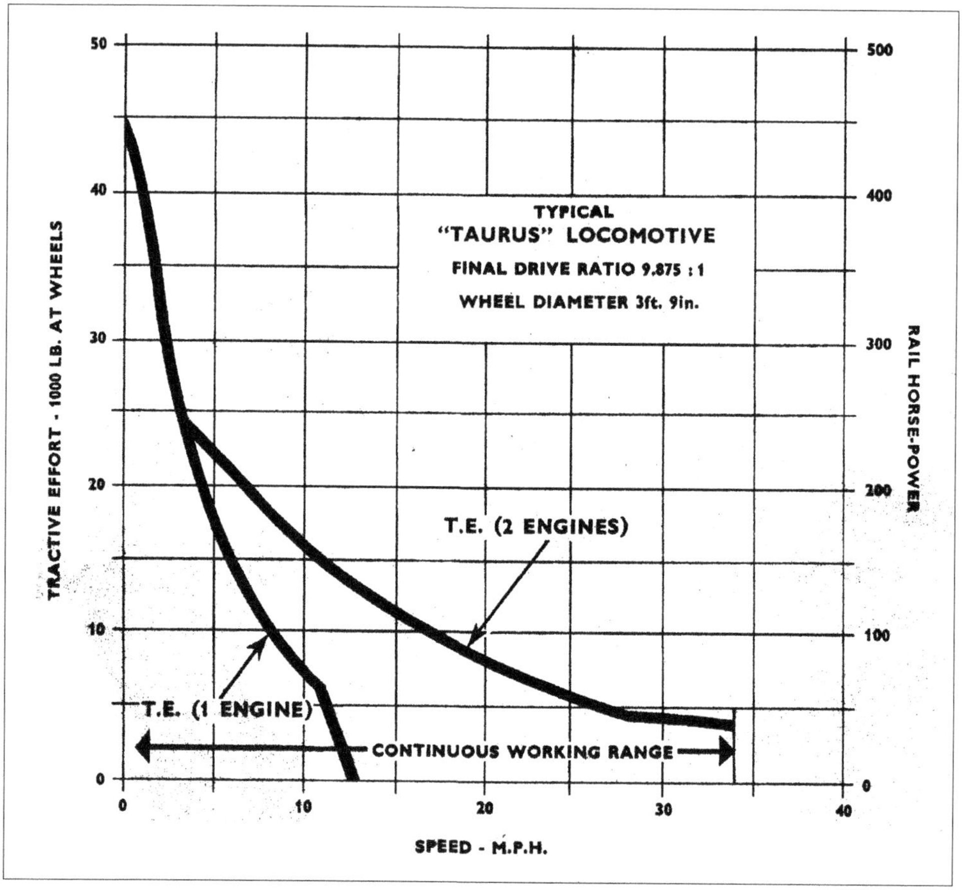

The graph compares the tractive effort and speed of the Taurus and shows how the second engine cuts in at about 3.5mph. (Rolls-Royce Specification)

Jack Christmas accompanied the Taurus locomotive (YE2892) to Spain. After setting the locomotive up at Naval works, the team took the locomotive to Madrid; Jack Christmas is second from the left. (Jack Christmas Collection)

In late 1962 the Yorkshire Engine Co. secured an order for a single Taurus for Spain's national railway RENFE. It was hoped that significant orders for perhaps forty or more locomotives might follow. The Taurus for the Spanish national railways was built to 5ft 6in gauge and was to be used primarily for building up passenger trains in Madrid. The locomotive was taken on a low loader to Liverpool for shipment to Bilbao in northern Spain and Jack Christmas, a Yorkshire Engine Co. Inspector, was flown out to Bilbao on 15 April 1963 to set the locomotive up in the Naval railway works and get it to Madrid. The ship arrived at Bilbao on 18 April and was offloaded once the paperwork was sorted. Matters proceeded slowly; RENFE inspected the Taurus on 6 May and permission was given to leave for Madrid on 11 May. A party of five accompanied the locomotive to Madrid – a Spanish inspector, guard and driver, a representative from Rolls-Royce and Jack Christmas from the Yorkshire Engine Co. A roundabout route was followed and the party had to find food where it could. On one occasion the driver returned from a local farmhouse with a pot of stew and a loaf of bread. Surprised that it tasted like seafood when they were so many miles from the sea, the driver advised that it had been a good year for snails in the local cemetery. It took Jack Christmas till 30 June to finalise delivery. Bureaucracy was considerable in Franco's Spain and, in spite of a follow-up visit by Compton during a holiday visit to Majorca, no more orders were forthcoming.[16] A factor which may have affected orders was a problem with the gear box. Yorkshire Engine Co. records show that the differential compounding gear box was changed to the simple compounding gear box used in the Indus, which in turn would have affected the speed and tractive effort of the locomotive and thereby changed its usefulness.[17] The Madrid Taurus effectively became an Indus and is now preserved in the transport museum in Madrid.

Orders from customers outside the United Kingdom were of significant importance to the Yorkshire Engine Co., particularly in its last three years. As in the past India and South America were the key regions.

The RENFE Taurus (YE2892) in operation near Madrid shortly after delivery; the locomotive is now in Museo Ferrocarril de Delicias, Madrid. (Jack Christmas Collection)

YORKSHIRE ENGINE OVERSEAS DIESEL CUSTOMERS

Customer	Locomotive Type	Nos	Delivery Dates
African Manganese – British Guyana	400hp Bo-Bo 3' 6 inch gauge based on Janus (3) 230hp 0-6-0 DE (1)	4	1958–9
Aluminium Union Port Esquivel Jamaica	Janus (1)	1	1959
BTH for Durgapur Steelworks	230hp 0-4-0 DE (10)	10	1958–9
Hindustan Steel	300hp 0-4-0 DE (5), 600hp Bo-Bo (10)	15	1963–4
Indian Fertilizer Corporation – Assam Division	Janus (2)	2	1963
RENFE	Taurus (1)	1	1963
Southern Railway Peru	350hp 0-6-0 DH (3)	3	1964
	Total	36	

A 3ft 6in-gauge Bo-Bo version of the Janus was developed for African Manganese's new mine in the north-west of British Guiana or Guyana, as the country is now called. Three of the Janus derivatives, plus one 230hp 0-6-0 DE had to be delivered by an indirect route. They were transported from the UK to Port Chagaramas in Trinidad. Here they were off-loaded onto a landing craft and carried 100 miles across the sea and up the Barima River to a point where they could be pulled onto the bank. From the landing point a track ran thirty miles to the mine. The locomotives had to haul 370 tons at an average speed of about 14mph. The steepest gradient was 1:100 and the journey was

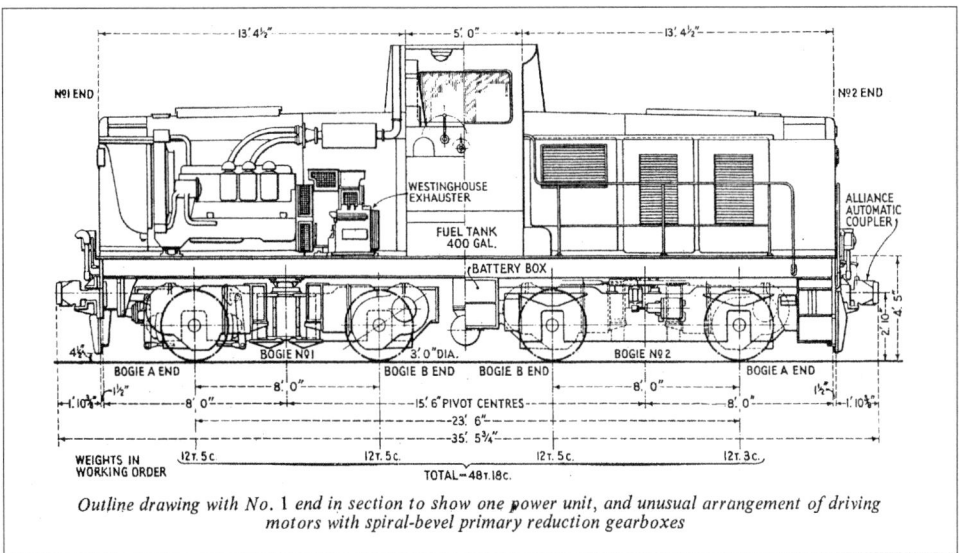

Outline drawing with No. 1 end in section to show one power unit, and unusual arrangement of driving motors with spiral-bevel primary reduction gearboxes

The Yorkshire Engine Co. supplied three 3ft 6in-gauge Bo-Bo versions of the Janus to the African Manganese Corporation's operations in Guyana in 1958–9 (YE2733–5). The line is now closed. (Drawing from January 1959 edition of the Railway Gazette*)*

expected to take three hours when loaded and 1½ hours when empty.[18] The mine is now closed and the line abandoned.

The Yorkshire Engine Co. had supplied several locomotives to Peru over the years, the last of which had been an oil-burning 0-6-0ST in 1952 to the Peruvian Corporation Ltd. The Southern Railway of Peru was one of six railways belonging to the Peruvian Corporation, one of the few South American lines still British controlled in the early 1960s. Three 350hp 0-6-0 DHs were despatched to Peru, one in April and two in June 1964. They used Rolls-Royce C8T engines and were priced at £19,430 each (YE2930–2932).

The Yorkshire Engine Co.'s first overseas orders had been for Indian railways and it was perhaps fitting that the last overseas order, nearly one hundred years later, should also go to India, albeit to an industrial customer. The Yorkshire Engine Co. had been given a contract by BTH in 1958 to build two batches of five 205hp 0-4-0 DEs (YE 2692–2696 and YE2697–2701) to assist with the construction phase of a new steelworks being built by a consortium of British companies at Durgapur. The engines were down-rated Rolls-Royce C6Ss. A £50,000 order followed in October 1962 from the Fertilizer Corporation of India for two metre-gauge Janus (YE2898 and YE2914), which were delivered in November 1963. The Yorkshire Engine Co.'s future for at least one more year was, however, secured in March 1963, when an order was received worth about £500,000 from Hindustan Steel for fifteen locomotives needed to operate the new Durgapur steelworks. This order for ten 600hp Bo-Bo DEs (YE2915–2924) and five four-wheel DEs (YE2925–2929) would keep the works occupied till early 1964. Each Bo-Bo cost £29,250 and each 300hp DE £15,144. The last three locomotives were delivered in July 1964, by which time the future of the Yorkshire Engine Co. was under discussion.[19]

As the Hindustan Steel locomotives were under construction, the Yorkshire Engine Co. brought out a brochure jointly with AEI (Formerly BTH) to promote Bo-Bo diesel electric locomotives. The version sold to India was named Olympus and available in a range of 500–800hp for 'heavy shunting and transfer duties' and in a weight range of 64–76 tons. Rolls-Royce, Cummins, Caterpillar or other engines could be fitted to suit the customer's preference. A 450–700hp lighter-weight version was also offered for 'shunting and light line services'. This version, called the Zeus, was to weigh between 48–60 tons, but was never built.[20]

The Southern Railway of Peru purchased three 0-6-0 DHs in 1964 at a price of £19,430 each, one in April and two in June 1964 (YE2930–32). (Derek Penney Collection)

YE2915 awaits despatch to Durgapur steelworks in India in December 1963; DL34 was the first of ten Olympus locomotives, which cost £29,520 each. (Howard Turner Collection)

A group of middle management outside the ambulance room at Meadowhall in the 1950s, with the nurse looking out of the window. Back row from left to right: -?-; J. Sweetman, Stock Controller; A. Marsden, Buyer; Edgar Knight, Erecting Shop Foreman; Joe Allen, Erecting Shop; -?-. Front row: H. Corbridge, Goods Received; Billy Smith, Boiler Shop Foreman. (Derek Penney Collection)

The Yorkshire Engine Co. sometimes worked with overseas locomotive builders. It produced special designs of some of its diesel hydraulic locomotives for both the 5ft 6in and metre gauges of Spain in both 0-4-0 and 0-6-0 versions. Twenty-nine metre-gauge locomotives were built under license at the Naval works at Sestao for six Spanish companies between 1965 and 1967. One of these locomotives can be seen at the Basque Railway Museum at Azpeitia.[21] The locomotives for the African Manganese Corporation in 1958–9 were based on a Bo-Bo diesel electric locomotive design built in South Africa. The Yorkshire Engine Co. also worked with a builder in Australia.[22]

Unlike the heads of other United Steel branches, the General Manager of Yorkshire Engine was not at first required to present a monthly report to the United Steel Managing Director's Advisory Committee (MDAC), although any Yorkshire Engine Co. capital expenditure had to be approved by this Committee. However, in early 1962 the policy changed and Watkin was required, with effect from March 1962, to deliver a monthly report to the MDAC. Financial performance and future orders were monitored. The MDAC were unhappy with Watkin's presentation of his forward order book and with the financial performance of the Yorkshire Engine Co. In January 1963 Peddie, the United Steel Co. Secretary was asked to talk to Watkin. The Committee noted that 'YE had been incurring manufacturing losses consistently during recent months'.[23]

Watkin's reports commented on orders for forgings and the machine shop as well as orders for locomotives. With the receipt of the Durgapur order in March 1963, the order book for locomotives was full and the machine shop and forge were busy. By November machinery orders had fallen off and many machines were idle. Once the Durgapur order had been completed, locomotive work was short and the MDAC looked to bring forward more United Steel orders to keep the works busy. An assessment was made of future locomotive requirements and the Committee reckoned in June 1964 that all United Steel requirements for locomotives could be met within eighteen months.

The senior management are lined up in front of a 200hp DH to mark the retirement of the Director's secretary, Miss Taylor. From left to right: Watson, Company Secretary; Compton, Technical Director; Miss Taylor; Watkin, General Manager; Bagguley, Works Manager. (Derek Penney Collection)

The Yorkshire Engine Co. attempted to reinvigorate its locomotive business by redesigning its locomotives in the summer and autumn of 1963. *Modern Transport* of 9 November 1963 carried photographs of a 0-6-0 of a new and more attractive design. 'It is bad publicity to have locomotives of untidy or eccentric appearance in the works yard even though they may be only momentarily visible to passers in main line expresses.' A leaflet was produced jointly with AEI to promote the Olympus and Zeus Bo-Bo Diesel Electric locomotives. A 0-6-0 DH with a 375hp Cummins engine was introduced. Such a redesign and strengthening of the range was not enough to win back sufficient customers to keep the works open, for other suppliers such as Sentinel had also produced more attractive modern designs By early 1964 most UK industrial plants had converted from steam to diesel. The British Railways network had reduced following the Beeching plan and the number of industrial sites requiring locomotives was falling. British Rail locomotives, including some of the Yorkshire Engine Co.'s own Class 02s were being sold off to industrial users. More plants were using road transport. United Steel, which had provided the Yorkshire Engine Co. with about 30 per cent of its diesel orders, had largely satisfied its own requirements for locomotive\s. The Yorkshire Engine Co.'s general engineering and overhaul business could not justify a works of the size of Meadowhall. Closure was inevitable, particularly when the plant could be more profitably used by another United Steel business.

An attempt was made during 1964 to stabilise production at a reduced level. This proved to be unsatisfactory. There could be overtime working in one area to meet an exceptional demand, whilst other departments were on short time. It was proving impossible to balance order books and the availability of specialist skills. A final decision was taken, probably in late 1964, to close the Yorkshire Engine Co.'s plant at Meadowhall and use the works for McCalls, United Steel's steel reinforcement business. Although the local management were denying closure was imminent, word had reached the Yorkshire Engine Co. from Appleby Frodingham and other branches by January 1965 that closure was planned.

Watkin and the United Steel head of labour relations, F.H. Larder, met unions, foremen and press at the end of February 1965 shortly after the news was broken to the staff. The *Sheffield Telegraph* headline of

This photograph of an unidentified 0-6-0 was used to accompany an article in Modern Transport in November 1963 announcing the Yorkshire Engine Co.'s new designs. (Jean Rose Collection)

This is believed to be one of two 375hp Cummins-engined 0-6-0s of modern design delivered to the NCB East Midlands division, one in August 1963 and a second in February 1964 (YE2910 or 2911). (Derek Penney Collection)

YE2940 was used at the NCB Calverton and is now being restored to full working order by Andrew Briddon at Peak Rail. (Andrew Briddon)

2 March 1965 read 'Rail Engine Firm Closing – Staff will not suffer'. The *Rotherham Advertiser* reported on 6 March 1965 'No sackings expected after Yorkshire Engine shutdown'. The MDAC was told that the announcements had met with no marked signs of disapproval. The workforce was already reduced to about 350 and United Steel was confident it could find work for the entire workforce at its branches. The workforce was told that, although the plant had had sales of £1 million in the last year, home orders would not be sufficient in the future. Even if overseas orders equivalent to those received from Durgapur could be obtained every year, they would not cover costs. Watkin commented on the temporary boost arising from the transfer from steam to diesel and added 'but as those (diesels) are built to last as long as thirty years, you can see that gradually demand slackened'. Watkin and Compton might have been both surprised and pleased that some of the Yorkshire Engine Co.'s locomotives were still at work fifty years after closure. In the year to September 1964, the last year for which accounts are available, the Yorkshire Engine Co. lost £34,099.

There were discussions between the Yorkshire Engine Co. management, the MDAC and the unions regarding payments to leavers. The United Steel Chairman wanted the same payment to be made to those who transferred internally as to those who left the United Steel group of companies. In the end it was agreed by the MDAC that internal transfers would receive £50. Leavers would in most cases get more. The scheme cost about £90,000. Opportunities in United Steel were plentiful, as the final phase of an £11.5 million project to expand electric arc steelmaking had just been opened at Steel, Peech & Tozer and plans were about to be announced for new steel-making plant at Samuel Fox at Stocksbridge. However, not all the Yorkshire Engine Co. workers were found suitable jobs locally and some preferred to take posts outside the United Steel group.

Peddie, the United Steel Co. Secretary, was charged with negotiating the sale to Rolls-Royce of the goodwill and name of the Yorkshire Engine Co. The Sentinel plant at Shrewsbury acquired the right to build locomotives to Yorkshire Engine Co. designs and received all the Yorkshire Engine Co. drawings. Three Janus were built at Shrewsbury for Appleby Frodingham, but only one remains in use. Rolls-Royce

YEC L122 was rebuilt by the new Yorkshire Engine Co. in 1993. The original English Electric D1198 was stripped down, running gear overhauled and a new engine and superstructure fitted. The locomotive still operates at Milford Haven in 2008. (Peter Briddon)

had a significant holding in Thomas Hill (Rotherham) Ltd, which had been building diesel locomotives under the Vanguard brand and selling Sentinel locomotives for Rolls-Royce. Alf Wood, Yorkshire Engine Co.'s Chief Draughtsman, joined Sentinel at Shrewsbury and Arthur Hunter, Yorkshire Engine Co.'s leading draughtsman, joined Thomas Hill, which also had copies of the Yorkshire Engine Co. diesel locomotive drawings, so that spares could continue to be provided and repair and maintenance work undertaken on Yorkshire Engine Co. locomotives.

The last Yorkshire Engine Co. report delivered to the MDAC in July 1965 suggested the shutdown was going to plan. It would seem all work had ceased by September 1965. Two completed locomotives remained unsold at the time, works numbers YE2895 and YE2896. Both were 220hp 0-6-0 DHs to the revised 1963 design. YE2895 had been used as a demonstrator and on loan to various sites. It was subsequently hired out and eventually sold by Thomas Hill. It survives in 2007 on the Elsecar Railway, near Barnsley. YE2896 remained at Meadowhall till the 1980s, where it was used by McCalls, the United Steel branch which took over the works. Compton died on 19 September 1965, a few days before his sixty-fifth birthday.

This might well have been the end of the Yorkshire Engine Co. story, but for Peter Briddon, who registered a new Yorkshire Engine Company on 29 December 1988. The trademarks had become available in 1985 and Peter Briddon, who had worked for Thomas Hill, decided there was a gap in the market which was no longer filled by Thomas Hill. He established an office in Rotherham and workshops at Long Marston in the Cotswolds. He was back in the business of major locomotive refurbishments by 1990 with a locomotive for the Channel Tunnel project. Over the subsequent ten years the business was successfully developed in the UK and interest grew in Europe. Unfortunately in August 2001 the bank suddenly withdrew funding and the company went into administration.[24]

As for the Yorkshire Engine Co. locomotives still in use in UK steelworks in 2008, their long-term future may be in doubt. Corus Northern Engineering Services announced in February 2007 its intention to build new 1,000hp industrial locomotives at Scunthorpe. The first four 100-ton locomotives are to

YEC L170 was rebuilt by the new Yorkshire Engine Co. in 2001 from Hunslet 9221. A new superstructure and cab were fitted, plus an engine to the customer's specification. It was in use at Ford's factory at Genk in Belgium till 2006. (Peter Briddon)

be used at the steel works at Port Talbot for transporting liquid metal. Corus at Appleby Frodingham are understood to be looking at replacements for their current fleet of elderly locomotives. Interested readers might like to take the opportunity offered by Appleby Frodingham Railway Preservation Society to tour the works by train and see Yorkshire Engine Co. locomotives in action around the steelworks while it is still possible.[25]

Notes

1. *Engineering*, 22 December 1961, p.820.
2. *Engineering*, 15 June 1956; also *Locomotive*, May 1956, p.81.
3. *Locomotive Magazine*, July 1958.
4. Rolls-Royce traction department publication No.16, November 1962.
5. *Engineering*, 22 December 1961, p.820.
6. *Times*, 30 August 1957.
7. *Railway Gazette*, 19 December 1958, p.739; *Locomotive*, January 1959, p.7.
8. Rolls-Royce Railway Traction Department Publication No.16, November 1962.
9. Discussion with Bernard Ledger, 16 August 2007.
10. *Modern Transport*, 15 December 1962.
11. Discussion with Bernard Ledger, 16 August 2007.
12. Discussion with Bernard Ledger, 16 August 2007.
13. www.traintesting.com/bulletin_12.htm
14. *The Diesel Shunter*, Colin Marsden, pp.124–5.
15. Taken from a Yorkshire Engine Co. Catalogue and quoted in *Engineering*, 12 May 1961.
16. Discussions with Jack Christmas and copies of his reports to Compton during his ten-week stay in Spain.
17. Yorkshire Engine Co. records via Andrew Briddon.
18. *Locomotive*, February 1959, p.27, and *Unisteel*, the United Steel newsletter, October 1964.
19. United Steel Managing Director's Advisory Committee minutes (MDAC), October 1962 and March 1963.
20. Brochure Ref. No.YEC 511 3½.6.63 in the collection of Derek Penney.
21. Museo Vasco del Ferrocarril, Azpeitia; see also Ferrocarriles.wikia.com/wiki/FEVE_Serie_1300.
22. United Steel Newsletter *Unisteel*, October 1964, p.3, article by Compton.
23. MDAC, January 1963.
24. Peter Briddon, December 2007.
25. Tours take place on Saturdays, sometimes behind a Yorkshire Engine Co. diesel, about once a month in winter and about twice a month in summer. More details can be found at www.afrps.co.uk or telephone 01652 657053.

Appendix A

Plan of Works

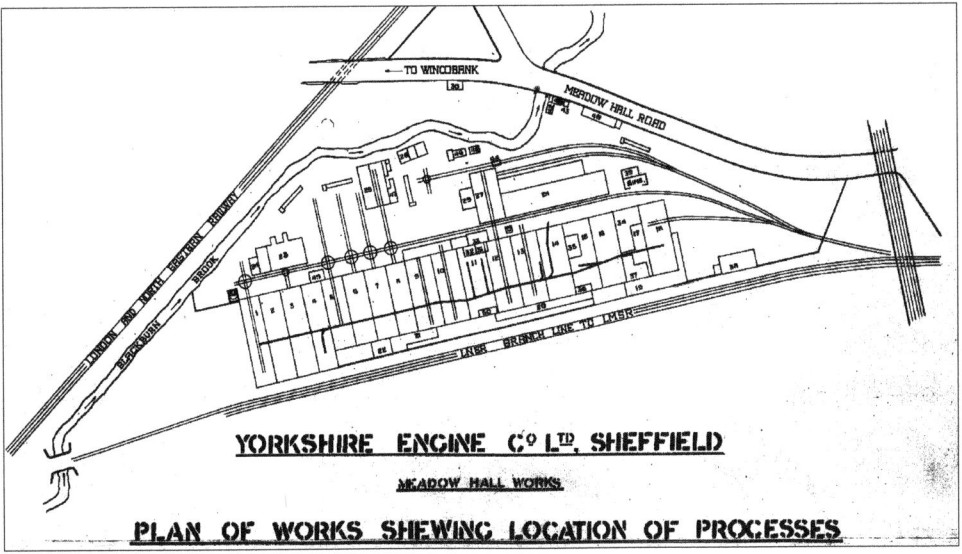

An undated plan of Meadowhall works prior to the United Steel's modernisation in 1950 shows the layout of the lines in the works. (Peter Hawkins Collection)

Appendix B

YORKSHIRE ENGINE ORDER BOOK

Steam, Electric and Tramway Locomotives

789 steam, electric and tramway locomotives built by the Yorkshire Engine Co. are listed below in works number order. A separate list is provided for diesel locomotives. Thirteen Yorkshire Engine Co. steam locomotives are thought to survive in 2008 and their works numbers are highlighted in bold. Additional information on the survivors is provided in the end notes. The list has been compiled from the order book in the Sheffield Archives and reviewed against a number of works lists held in the Stephenson Locomotive Society Library. The Yorkshire Engine Co. drew up the list now in the Sheffield Archives in about 1905, probably from the more comprehensive Drawing Office order books also held in the Sheffield Archives. The Yorkshire Engine Co. allocated contract and works numbers to boilers, cranes, coal cutters, haulage engines and other items, but these are not listed. The list may contain errors.

The Yorkshire Engine Co. often made standard industrial locomotives to stock. Where several industrial locomotives are listed together, these are likely to be a stock order e.g. 179-182, 235–238, 257–262, 284–289.

Customer	Works Number	Year	Nos	Type	Gauge
Great Northern	1–3	1866–7	3	2-4-0	Standard
East Indian	4–21 22–33	1867 1868	30	0-6-0	5ft 6in
Great Indian Peninsula	34–53	1868–9	20	0-6-0	5ft 6in
Great Northern	54–63	1868	10	2-4-0	Standard
Fairbairn Engineering	64–67	1867	4	0-6-0	5ft 3in
Midland	68–77	1868–9	10	0-6-0	Standard
Jamaica via Fairbairn	78–79	1868	2	2-4-0T	Standard
Tambov-Koslov	80–87	1869	8	0-6-0	5ft
Tambov-Koslov	88–91	1869	4	2-4-0	5ft
Lemberg Czernowitz	92–97	1869	6	0-6-0	Standard
Poti-Tiflis	98–107	1869	10	0-6-4T	5ft
Poti-Tiflis	108–117	1869	10	0-4-4T	5ft
Earl Fitzwilliam	118–120	1869	3	0-4-0ST	Standard
Moscow-Ryazan	121–128	1870	8	0-6-0	5ft
Buenos Ayres Great Southern	129–131	1870	3	4-4-0	5ft 6in
Poti-Tiflis	132–146	1870	15	0-6-4T	5ft
Poti-Tiflis	147–149	1870	3	0-4-4T	5ft
Stanton Iron	150	1870	1	0-6-0ST	Standard
Belfast Holywood & Bangor	151–152	1870	2	2-4-0T	5ft 3in
Victorian Railways	153–158	1871	6	0-6-0	5ft 3in
Monmouthshire	159–160	1871	2	0-6-0T	Standard
Neath & Brecon	161	1871	1	4-4-0T	Standard
Kiveton Park Colliery Wingerworth Iron	162 163	1871	2	0-4-0ST	Standard
Imperial Japanese[1]	**164**	1871	1	2-4-0T	3ft 6in
Darfield Main Colliery	165	1871	1	0-4-0ST	Standard
Buenos Ayres Great Southern[2] (**168**)	166–169	1871	4	2-4-0T	5ft 6in
Mexican Railway	170–174	1872	5	0-6-6-0F[3]	Standard
Nitrate Railway	175	1874	1	0-6-6-0F	Standard
Hallsberg-Motola-Mjobly	176–177	1874	2	0-4-4-0F	Standard
Canto-Gallo	178	1873	1	0-4-4-0F	3ft 7 1/4in
Charles Cammell Craik Brown Bayley Thomas Vickers	179 180 181 182	1872	4	0-4-0ST	Standard
Buenos Ayres Great Southern	183–184	1872	2	2-4-0T	5ft 6in
Potteries, Shrewsbury & North Wales	185	1872	1	2-4-0T	Standard
Compostelano	186–189	1872	4	0-6-0T	5ft 6in

Name	Numbers	Date	Qty	Wheel arr.	Gauge
Mexican	190–194	1873	5	0-6-6-0F	Standard
Great Eastern	195–209	1872–3	15	0-6-0	Standard
Peruvian	210–211	1873	2	0-4-0ST	3ft 6in
Luxembourg	212	1872	1	0-6-6-0F	Standard
Luxembourg	213–218	1873	6	0-6-0	Standard
Poti-Tiflis or Nitrate[4]	219	1874 or later	1	0-6-6-0F	–
Poti-Tiflis	220–223		4	0-6-6-0F	5ft
Nitrate Railway	224–228		5	2-6-6-2F	Standard
Buenos Ayres Great Southern	229–234	1874	6	4-4-0	5ft 6in
W. Cooke	235	1874	4	0-4-0ST	Standard
W. Bacon	236				
W. Jessop	237				
J. Summers	238				
New Zealand[5] (**241** & **244**)	239–249	1874	11	0-6-0ST	3ft 6in
Imperial Ottoman	250–254	1874	5	0-6-0	1100m
New Zealand	255–256	1875	2	0-4-0T	3ft 6in
Appleby Iron	257	1875/6	6	0-4-0ST	Standard
Featherstone Main	258				
Ashbury's Carriage	259				
Brown Bayley Dixon	260				
Darfield Main	261				
T. Charlton	262				
Lancashire & Yorkshire	263–274	1875–6	12	0-6-0	Standard
Buenos Ayres GS	275–278	1875	4	4-4-0 5ft 6	3ft 6in
Benton & Woodwiss	279–281	1876	3	0-4-0-ST	Standard
Chatterley Iron	282–283	1876	2	0-4-0ST	Standard
Benton and Woodwiss	284	1876–7	6	0-4-0ST	Standard
Goldendale Iron	285				
Hoyland Silkstone	286				
Jackson Gill	287				
Chas Cammell	288–9				
San Juan de Las Abedesas	290–292	1876	3	0-8-0-T	5ft 6in
Indian State Railways	293–318	1876–7	26	0-6-0	Metre
J. Taylor	319	1877–1880	6	0-4-0ST	Standard
Wilson Cammell	320				
Carnforth Iron	321				
Steel Tozer & Hamilton	322				
Skinner & Hilford	323				
Thos. Peake	324				
New Hucknall	325	1878–1882	3	0-6-0ST	Standard
Chatterley Iron	326				
Naylor Bros	327				
Felixstowe Rail & Pier	328–330	1877	3	2-4-0T	Standard
East Indian Railway	331–355	1877	25	0-6-0	5ft 6in
Hoylake & Birkenhead	356–357	1877	2	2-4-0T	Standard
Tramway Locomotives[6]	358–359	1878	2	0-4-0	Standard

Wharncliffe Silkstone	361	1880	1	0-4-0ST	1ft 8
S. Fox	364	1880	1	0-4-0T	Standard
Mexican Railway	365–367	1883	3	0-6-6-0F	Standard
Sharp Stewart for Nitrate Railway	368–371	1883	4	2-6-0T	Standard
Buenos Ayres Great Southern	378–382	1884	5	0-6-0T	5ft 6in
Sharp Stewart	388–390	-	3	2-4-0	Standard
South Indian Railway	399–402	1885	4	0-4-4T	Metre
FC Compostelano	403	-	1	0-6-0T	5ft 6in
HM War Office[7]	404–405	1885	2	0-4-2T	2ft 6in
Truman Hanbury Buxton J. Grayson Lowood	406 407	1886 1887	2	0-4-0ST	Standard
Charles Cammell	414	1886	1	0-4-0ST	Standard
Charles Cammell	425–6	1888	2	0-4-0ST	Standard
Nitrate Railways	427	-	1	0-4-0ST	Standard
Southern Coal NSW	428–429	1888	2	0-6-0ST	Standard
Mexican Southern	435–436	-	2	0-6-0ST	3ft
Charles Cammell	441	1890	1	0-4-0ST	Standard
Nitrate Railways	442–443	1890	2	0-6-6-0F	Standard
Anglo Chilean Nitrate & Railway Co.	446–447	1891	2	0-6-6-0F	3ft 6in
Wharncliffe Silkstone	450	1890	1	0-4-0ST	1ft 8in
HM War Office	462	1891	1	0-4-4T	2 6in
Bombay Baroda & Central India Railway – H.H. Gaekwar's State Railway	463–464	1891	2	0-4-2	2ft 6in
HM War Office	468	1890	1	4w electric	-
Wharncliffe Woodmoor Chatterley Whitfield	469 470	1891	2	0-4-0ST	Standard
John Brown Wharncliffe Silkstone Leeds Forge Wath Main	478 479 480 481	1891–2	4	0-4-0ST	Standard
Wharncliffe Silkstone Wm Wood Hoyland Silkstone John Brown	483 484 485 486	1895–6	4	0-4-0ST	Standard
Bombay Baroda & Central India	528–530	1896	3	0-4-2	2ft 6in
Queensland Government Railway[8] (**532**)	531–540	1896–7	10	4-6-0	3ft 6in
Nunnery Colliery	546	1897	1	0-4-0T	2ft 4in
Hull & Barnsley	547–552	1897	6	0-6-0	Standard
HM War Office	554–5	1898	2	0-6-0T	Metre
Moira Colliery	559	1898	1	0-4-0ST	Standard
Hull & Barnsley	560–562	1898	3	0-6-0	Standard
Sharp Stewart for Sao Paulo	567–569	1898	3	0-4-0ST	5ft 3in

Thomas Peake Preston Coal Burradon & Coxlodge	580 581 582	1899	3	0-4-0ST	
Hull & Barnsley	604–609	1900	6	0-6-0	Standard
Wharncliffe Silkstone Vickers Sons Maxim Ashburys' Carriage	610 611 612	1900	3	0-4-0ST	Standard
Metropolitan Railway	624–627	1901	4	0-6-2T	Standard
Frodingham Iron Charles Cammell William Jessop	628 629 630	1901–2	3	0-4-0ST	Standard
Hull & Barnsley	655–660	1900	6	0-6-0ST	Standard
HM War Office[9]	711	1902	1	0-6-2T	2ft 6in
Bombay Baroda & Central India	723–729	1902	7	0-6-0	5ft 6in
HM War Office[10]	757	1904	1	2-6-2ST	2ft 6in
Great Central	765–769	1904	5	0-6-0	Standard
Parkgate Charles Cammell	784 785	1905	2	0-4-0ST	Standard
Junin Railway	791–792	1904	2	0-6-2ST	2ft 6in
Hepworth Iron	799	1905	1	0-6-0ST	Standard
Great Central	820–824	1905	5	0-6-0	Standard
Steel Peech & Tozer	832	1905	1	0-4-0ST	Standard
Junin Railway	834–835	1905	2	0-6-6-0F	2ft 6in
Great Central	854–858	1906	5	0-6-0	Standard
Nunnery Colliery	898	1906	1	0-4-0ST	2ft 4in
Hull and Barnsley	899–908	1907	10	0-8-0	Standard
Nitrate Railways	940–941	1907	2	0-6-6-0T	Standard
Hull & Barnsley	942–946	1907	5	0-8-0	Standard
Goldendale Iron Bolsover Colliery	947 948	1907 1908	2	0-4-0ST	Standard
Josiah Hardman W.M. Cooke	1011 1012	1908 1909	2	0-4-0ST	Standard
Rothervale Colliery Newbiggin	1021 1022	1909–10	2	0-6-0ST	Standard
Hoyland Silkstone	1023	1909	1	0-4-0ST	Standard
Hoyland Silkstone T.W. Ward	1026 1027	1910–2	2	0-4-0ST	Standard
North British Railway	1066–1095	1911–3	30	4-4-2T	Standard
Puerto Cabello & Valencia	1096	1911	1	0-4-0ST	3ft 6in
Callenders Cable	1135	1912	1	0-4-0ST	3ft 6in
Hull & Barnsley	1182–1186	1914	5	0-6-0	Standard
Midland Coal Coke David Colville	1275–6 1277	1915	3	0-6-0ST	Standard
Metropolitan	1283–1284	1915	2	0-6-4T	Standard

Indian State Railways United Provinces	1285–1287	1915	3	0-6-0T	2ft
South Indian Railway	1288–1294	1919	7	0-4-4BT	Metre
Tirdonkin Shirebrook	1299 1300	1916	2	0-6-0ST	Standard
Metropolitan	1301–1302	1916	2	0-6-4T	Standard
Midland Coal Coke & Iron	1356	1917	1	0-6-0ST	Standard
Maryport & Carlisle	1582–1583	1921	2	0-6-0	Standard
Babcock y Wilcox, Bilbao	1658	1921	1	4-8-0	5ft 6in
Hatfield Main Tirdonkin	1787 1788	1922	2	0-6-0ST	Standard
Wath Main	1823	1923	1	0-6-0ST	Standard
Derwent Valley water board	1878	1921	1	0-4-0ST	Standard
Henry Boot & Sons	1887–1888	1922	2	0-4-0T	2ft
Barnsley Main Measham Collieries	1889 1890	1923–4	2	0-6-0ST	Standard
Hoyland Silkstone	1891	1923	1	0-4-0ST	Standard
Nitrate Railways	1941–1946	1923–4	6	4-8-4T	Standard
Baburizza & Co.	1947	1923	1	0-4-2T	Metre
Bengal Nagpur	1992–1995	1924	4	2-8-2	2ft 6in
Central Railway of Peru	2038–2042	1925	5	4-8-2	Standard
Lobitos Development Rly	2093–2094	1925	2	0-4-2T	2ft 6in
Appleby Iron Co.	2140–2142	1927	3	0-6-0ST	Standard
Haunchwood Brick & Tile	2196	1930	1	0-4-0ST	Standard
New Hucknall	2197	1928	1	0-6-0ST	Standard
LNER	2220–2228	1928–9	9	0-6-2T	Standard
Ravenglass & Eskdale	2229	1928	1	2-8-2+0-8-0	1ft 3in
United Steel Rothervale	2240–2241	1929	2	0-6-0ST	Standard
GWR Pannier Tank	2249–2273	1930	25	0-6-0	Standard
Romney Hythe & Dymchurch[11] (**2294.5**)	2294–2295	1931	2	4-6-2	1ft 3in
Wath Main New Hucknall	2306 2307	1931 1931	2	0-6-0ST	Standard
Eastern Bengal[12] (**2320**)	2320–2322	1932–3	3	2-4-0T	2ft 6in
Sandwith & Clugston Slag	2340	1934	1	0-6-0ST	Standard
Steel Peech & Tozer	2343–2345	1934	3	0-4-0ST	Standard
Steel Peech & Tozer	2361	1935	1	0-4-0ST	Standard
Sheffield Corp. Electricity	2374	1937	1	0-4-0ST	Standard
Steel Peech & Tozer	2383–2384	1937	2	0-4-0ST	Standard
Sheffield Corp. Electricity	2403	1941	1	0-4-0ST	Standard
Clayton Equipment for Capenhurst Ordnance Factory	2404	1941	1	Battery Electric	Standard
Steetley Lime & Basic	2407	1942	1	0-4-0ST	Standard

Clayton Equipment for Warwickshire Electric works	2411	1943	1	0-4-0 Electric Trolley	Standard
Sheepbridge Coal & Iron	2413	1943	1	0-6-0ST	Standard
Clayton Equipment for ICI Billingham	2414	1944	1	Electric Trolley	–
Appleby Frodingham	2422–2423	1947	2	0-6-0ST I[13]	Standard
Workington Harbour & Dock	2425	1947	1	0-4-0STV[14]	Standard
Appleby Frodingham	2426–2428	1948	3	0-6-0ST I	Standard
Workington Harbour & Dock NCB Northern Division	2429 2430-2	1948	4	0-4-0ST IV[15]	Standard
United Steel Ore Appleby Frodingham	2433 2434	1948	2	0-6-0ST I	Standard
United Coke & Chemicals	2435	1948	1	0-4-0ST IV	Standard
United Coke & Chemicals Appleby Frodingham Samuel Fox	2438 2439 2440	1949	3	0-6-0ST I	Standard
Appleby Frodingham	2442	1949	1	0-6-0ST I	Standard
Western Region Pannier Tank	2443–2472	1949–52	30	0-6-0T	Standard
NCB South Barnsley[16]	2473-**2474**	1949	2	0-4-0 STV	Standard
Steel Peech & Tozer	2475	1949	1	0-4-0STV	Standard
Appleby Frodingham	2476–2478	1949	3	0-6-0ST I	Standard
Samuel Fox	2479	1949	1	0-6-0ST I	Standard
United Steel Ore Mining	2483–2484	1950	2	0-6-0ST I	Standard
Samuel Fox	2485	1950	1	0-6-0ST I	Standard
Appleby Frodingham	2486	1949	1	0-6-0ST I	Standard
United Steel Ore Mining	2487	1950	1	0-6-0ST I	Standard
Appleby Frodingham	2488	1950	1	0-6-0ST I	Standard
United Steel Ore Mining	2489	1950	1	0-6-0ST I	Standard
Samuel Fox[17]	**2498**	1951	1	0-6-0ST I	Standard
Lancashire Steel Irlam	2499	1951	1	0-6-0ST I	Standard
United Steel Ore Mining	2500	1951	1	0-6-0ST I	Standard
United Steel Ore Mining	2501–2	1951	2	0-6-0ST I	Standard
United Steel Ore Mining	2510	1952	1	0-6-0ST I	Standard
Peruvian Corporation	2511	1952	1	0-6-0ST I	Standard
United Steel Ore Mining	2512	1952	1	0-6-0ST I	Standard
Central Railway Paraguay	**2513-4**[18]	1953	2	2-6-0	Standard
App Frodingham[19] (**2521**)	2520–2523	1952	4	0-6-0ST I	Standard
United Coke & Chemicals	2524	1952	1	0-6-0ST I	Standard
British Railways via Hunslet	2544–2553	1954–5	10	0-6-0 Pannier	Standard
Chilean Northern (Antofagasta & Bolivia)	2554–5	1955	2	2-8-2	Metre
United Coke & Chemicals	2562	1954	1	0-6-0ST I	Standard
United Steel Ore Mining	2563–4	1954	2	0-6-0ST I	Standard

United Steel Ore Mining	2566	1955	1	0-6-0ST A[20]	Standard
United Steel Ore Mining	2567–2569	1955	3	0-6-0ST A	Standard
United Steel Ore Mining	2570–2572	1955	3	0-6-0ST A	Standard
United Coke & Chemicals	2573	1955	1	0-6-0ST A	Standard
British Railways via Hunslet	2575–2584	1955–56	10	0-6-0 Pannier Tank	Standard
Workington Harbour Workington Iron & Steel Workington Harbour	2585 2586 2587	1955	3	0-4-0ST V	Standard
Workington Iron and Steel	2602	1955	1	0-4-0ST V	Standard
			789		

Notes

1. YE164 survives as an exhibit at Oume Railway Park, Japan.
2. YE168 is displayed on a plinth at St Raphael, Mendoza, Argentina.
3. Fairlie patent locomotives are marked F on this list.
4. The records are incomplete. The first locomotive completed (YE219) may have gone to Pisagua for the Nitrate Railway but some commentators suggest it went to the Poti-Tiflis and was lost at sea; YE220–223 went to the Poti-Tiflis after conversion to 5ft gauge; 224–228 were modified by Fairlie to 2-6-6-2 and sent to the Nitrate Railway, which was the original customer for all ten locomotives, in 1882.
5. YE241 is stored for parts at Ferrymead, NZ and YE244 is undergoing restoration on the Western Springs Railway at the Museum of Transport & Technology, NZ.
6. The Belgian Street Railway ordered a tramway locomotive in October 1873. It was not given a works number and is not included in this list. Works numbers YE358–9 appear to have been reserved for tramway locomotives ordered by Edward Sacré with board approval and without a designated customer. Board minutes mention the despatch of two tramway locomotives to Barcelona, which are assumed to be YE358–9.
7. Chattenden & Upnor Railway, later called Lodge Hill & Upnor.
8. YE532 is stored at the Ipswich Railway Workshops, Queensland, Australia.
9. Lodge Hill & Upnor Railway.
10. Lodge Hill & Upnor Railway.
11. Both locomotives survive and are in frequent use on the Romney Hythe & Dymchurch Railway.
12. YE2320 is on a plinth at the Eastern Railway headquarters in Calcutta.
13. I Indicates a Type I locomotive based on a United Steel specification, which drew on a Stephenson design.
14. V indicates a standard YE design Type V locomotive.
15. IV indicates a standard YE Type IV locomotive.
16. YE2474 is located at the Embsay & Bolton Abbey Railway.
17. YE2498 is kept at Buckinghamshire Rail Centre, Quainton Road.
18. Both locomotives survive at the workshops of the Central Paraguay Railway; 2513 is steamed occasionally.
19. YE2521 is owned by the National Mining Museum and is based at Roacks by Rail, Cottesmore, Rutland.
20. A indicates an Austerity design using Hunslet drawings.

Appendix C

YORKSHIRE ENGINE ORDER BOOK

Diesel Locomotives

This list of 377 locomotives was drawn from the order book and the Yorkshire Engine Company drawing office diesel list held in the Sheffield Archives. It has been reviewed against other lists, but errors may remain, particularly with regard to the last locomotives built. Some may have been completed elsewhere. The list excludes Yorkshire Engine designed locomotives made by Rolls Royce following the closure of Meadowhall, those made under licence overseas and the locomotives of the 1988 Yorkshire Engine Company.

Sixty-one Yorkshire Engine diesel locomotives are thought to survive on operational sites or preserved railways in the UK in July 2014. Some of these are out of use or held for replacement parts. A Taurus is preserved in Madrid, and the remains of 230hp diesel electric locomotive were seen in Guyana within the last two years. The works numbers for these survivors are highlighted in **bold**. Readers are advised to make checks before arranging a visit, as locomotives are often moved between sites

Janus YE2641 ex-Port of London Authority when at Rutland Railway Museum. (Andrew Hurrell)

YE2672 ex-Brightside Foundry at Churnet Valley Railway. (Andrew Hurrell)

YE2676 ex-Staveley Iron & Chemical at Bombardier Crewe. (Andrew Hurrell)

YE2688 was the only surviving DE2; recently at the Rutland Railway Museum, it was scrapped in August 2008. (Andrew Hurrell)

Janus YE2868 ex-Shelton Iron at Foxfield Railway. (Andrew Hurrell)

YE2872 ex-United Steel ore mining branch at Rutland Railway Museum awaiting restoration. (Andrew Hurrell)

Works number	HP	Whs.	Type	Customer and where in use or preserved	Month	Year
2480	250	0-4-0	DE	Steel, Peech & Tozer at Peak Rail	12	50
2481	250	0-4-0	DE	Steel, Peech & Tozer at Kelham Island Museum, Sheffield	2	51
2504	275	0-4-0	DE2	Lancashire Steel	3	53
2505	275	0-4-0	DE2	Stewarts &Lloyds Bilston	3	53
2506	275	0-4-0	DE2	Stewarts &Lloyds Bilston	4	53
2507	275	0-4-0	DE2	Stewarts &Lloyds Bilston	5	53
2508	275	0-4-0	DE2	Stewarts &Lloyds Bilston	12	53
2509	275	0-4-0	DE2	Stewarts &Lloyds Bilston	1	54
2527	400	0-6-0	DE4	John Summers	11	53
2528	400	0-6-0	DE4	Samuel Fox	2	54
2529	275	0-4-0	DE2	Samuel Fox	5	54
2530	275	0-4-0	DE2	Steel Peech & Tozer	3	54
2531	275	0-4-0	DE2	Steel Peech & Tozer	5	54
2532	275	0-4-0	DE2	Lancashire Steel	4	54
2533	275	0-4-0	DE2	Lancashire Steel	7	54
2588	275	0-4-0	DE2	Steel Peech & Tozer	4	55
2589	275	0-4-0	DE2	Lancashire Steel	5	55
2590	275	0-4-0	DE2	Lancashire Steel	5	55
2591	275	0-4-0	DE2	Lancashire Steel	6	55
2592	275	0-4-0	DE2	Lancashire Steel	9	55
2593	275	0-4-0	DE2	Round Oak Brierley Hill	12	55
2594	400	0-6-0	Janus	Appleby Frodingham at Tata Aldwarke	3	56
2595	400	0-6-0	Janus	Appleby Frodingham	8	56
2596	275	0-4-0	DE2	Stanton Iron	1	56
2597	275	0-4-0	DE2	Stanton Iron	1	56
2598	275	0-4-0	DE2	Stanton Iron	3	56
2599	275	0-4-0	DE2	Lancashire Steel	12	55
2600	275	0-4-0	DE2	Lancashire Steel	4	56
2601	275	0-4-0	DE2	Lancashire Steel	7	56
2603	200	0-6-0	DE	Distington Engineering	10	55
2604	200	0-6-0	DE	Brymbo	1	56
2605	400	0-6-0	DE4	NCB	9	55
2606	400	0-6-0	DE4	Samuel Fox	12	55
2607	400	0-6-0	DE4	Samuel Fox	9	56
2608	400	0-6-0	DE4	Samuel Fox	12	56
2609	235	0-4-0	DE	ICI	7	56
2610	235	0-4-0	DE	ICI	7	56
2611	235	0-4-0	DE	ICI	8	56

2612	235	0-4-0	DE	ICI	9	56
2613	235	0-4-0	DE	ICI	11	56
2614	275	0-4-0	DE	Round Oak	2	57
2615	275	0-4-0	DE	Lancashire Steel	2	57
2616	275	0-4-0	DE	Lancashire Steel	3	57
2617	275	0-6-0	DE	North West Gas	5	58
2618	275	0-6-0	DE	North West Gas	5	58
2619	400	0-6-0	Janus	PLA[1]	11	56
2620	400	0-6-0	Janus	PLA	11	56
2621	200	0-4-0	DE	Stanton Iron	11	56
2622	200	0-4-0	DE	Stanton Iron		56
2623	200	0-4-0	DE	Stanton Iron	12	56
2624	200	0-4-0	DE	Stanton Iron	1	57
2625	200	0-4-0	DE	Stanton Iron	1	57
2626	200	0-4-0	DE	Pilkington	1	57
2627	200	0-4-0	DE	Darwen & Mostyn Iron at Mostyn Docks	2	57
2628	200	0-4-0	DE	Workington Harbour at Caledonian Railway, Angus	10	57
2629	400	0-6-0	Janus	ICI	11	57
2630	400	0-6-0	Janus	PLA at Llangollen Railway	5	57
2631	200	0-4-0	DE	Clugston Cawood	2	57
2632	200	0-4-0	DE	Brymbo	3	57
2633	400	0-6-0	Janus	PLA	5	57
2634	400	0-6-0	Janus	Appleby Frodingham	5	57
2635	400	0-6-0	Janus	Appleby Frodingham at Tata Stocksbridge	5	57
2636	275	0-4-0	DE2	Lancashire Steel	6	57
2637	275	0-4-0	DE2	Lancashire Steel	6	57
2638	275	0-4-0	DE2	Lancashire Steel	7	57
2639	275	0-4-0	DE2	Lancashire Steel	7	57
2640	400	0-6-0	Janus	PLA	6	57
2641	400	0-6-0	Janus	PLA at Blatchford Light Railway, Somerset	6	57
2642–2651	800	-	Bo-Bo	For British Transport Commission via BTH[2]	-	57–58
2652	200	0-4-0	DE	Steetley Oughtibridge Silica Firebrick	7	57
2653	200	0-4-0	DE	Pilkington	8	57
2654	200	0-4-0	DE	Pilkington at Nene Valley Railway	8	57
2655	200	0-4-0	DE	Lancashire Steel	8	57
2656	200	0-4-0	DE	Workington Iron & Steel	10	57
2657	200	0-4-0	DE	Workington Iron & Steel	10	57
2658	200	0-6-0	DE	Brymbo	10	57
2659	200	0-6-0	DE	Brymbo	10	57
2660	200	0-6-0	DE	NCB North Western Division		58

2661	200	0-6-0	DE	Eccles Slag at Appleby Frodingham Railway Preservation Society (AFRPS), Scunthorpe	1	59
2662	275	0-4-0	DE2	Round Oak	12	57
2663	275	0-4-0	DE2	Stewarts & Lloyds	2	58
2664	275	0-4-0	DE2	Steel Peech & Tozer	1	58
2665	400	0-6-0	Janus	ICI	12	57
2666	400	0-6-0	Janus	ICI	12	57
2667	400	0-6-0	Janus	Samuel Fox	11	57
2668	400	0-6-0	Janus	Appleby Frodingham	5	58
2669	400	0-6-0	Janus	Appleby Frodingham	4	58
2670	400	0-6-0	Janus	Stanton Iron at Stainmore Rsailway, Kirkby Stephen East	9	58
2671	400	0-6-0	Janus	Samuel Fox	11	57
2672	167	0-4-0	DH	Brightside Foundry at Churnet Valley Railway, Leek	5	60
2673	170	0-4-0	DH	CEGB Yorkshire Division	8	59
2674	220	0-4-0	DH	NCB Wakefield Area £9,000	3	63
2675	220	0-4-0	DH	South Yorkshire Chemicals at Peak Rail, Derbyshire	6	61
2676	220	0-4-0	DH	Staveley Iron & Chemicals at Brodie Engineering, East Ayrshire	12	59
2677	170	0-4-0	DH	Pilkington at Ribble Steam	5	60
2678	220	0-4-0	DH	NCB	12	61
2679	220	0-4-0	DH	South Yorkshire Chemicals at Peak Rail	4	62
2680	200	0-4-0	DE	Steel Peech & Tozer	2	58
2681	200	0-4-0	DE	Steel Peech & Tozer	2	58
2682	200	0-4-0	DE	Steel Peech & Tozer	3	58
2683	200	0-4-0	DE	Lancashire Steel	2	58
2684	200	0-4-0	DE	Workington Harbour & Dock at Caledonian Railway, Angus	5	58
2685	200	0-4-0	DE	Workington Iron & Steel	6	58
2686	200	0-4-0	DE	Esso	5	58
2687	200	0-4-0	DE	Pilkington at Telford Steam Railway	6	58
2688	275	0-4-0	DE2	Steel Peech & Tozer	7	59
2689	275	0-4-0	DE2	Workington Iron & Steel	8	59
2690	400	0-6-0	Janus	PLA at Tata Scunthorpe	5	59
2691	400	0-6-0	Janus	PLA	5	59
2692	230	0-4-0	DE	BTH for Durgapur	8	58
2693	230	0-4-0	DE	BTH for Durgapur	8	58
2694	230	0-4-0	DE	BTH for Durgapur	9	58
2695	230	0-4-0	DE	BTH for Durgapur	9	58
2696	230	0-4-0	DE	BTH for Durgapur	9	58

2697	230	0-4-0	DE	BTH for Durgapur	2	59
2698	230	0-4-0	DE	BTH for Durgapur	2	59
2699	230	0-4-0	DE	BTH for Durgapur	2	59
2700	230	0-4-0	DE	BTH for Durgapur	3	59
2701	230	0-4-0	DE	BTH for Durgapur	4	59
2702	275	0-4-0	DE	Stewarts & Lloyds	7	58
2703	275	0-4-0	DE	Lancashire Steel	7	58
2704	275	0-4-0	DE	Workington Iron & Steel	8	58
2705	275	0-4-0	DE	Stanton Iron	9	58
2706	275	0-4-0	DE	Stanton Iron	9	58
2707	275	0-4-0	DE2	Lancashire Steel	11	58
2708	400	0-6-0	Janus	NCB Northern Division	3	59
2709	400	0-6-0	Janus	United Steels Ore Mining at Tata Scunthorpe	4	59
2710	275	0-4-0	DE2	Steel Peech & Tozer	8	59
2711	275	0-4-0	DE2	Workington Iron & Steel	2	60
2712	400	0-6-0	Janus	NCB	6	58
2713	400	0-6-0	Janus	NCB	6	58
2714	400	0-6-0	Janus	ICI at Europee Metal Recycling, South Yorkshire	6	58
2715	400	0-6-0	Janus	AF	3	58
2716	400	0-6-0	Janus	AF	3	58
2717	400	0-6-0	Janus	NCB	7	58
2718	400	0-6-0	Janus	ICI at West Coast Railway, Carnforth	7	58
2719	400	0-6-0	Janus	ICI	7	58
2720	400	0-6-0	Janus	Samuel Fox	10	58
2721	400	0-6-0	Janus	Samuel Fox	10	58
2722	400	0-6-0	Janus	Samuel Fox	11	58
2723	400	0-6-0	Janus	ICI	11	58
2724	400	0-6-0	Janus	ICI	11	58
2725	400	0-6-0	Janus	ICI at Faber Prest Flixborough	11	58
2726	400	0-6-0	Janus	Aluminium Union Jamaica	2	59
2727	400	0-6-0	Janus	Appleby Frodingham	3	59
2728	400	0-6-0	Janus	Appleby Frodingham	2	59
2729	200	0-4-0	DE	Barnsley District Coking	12	58
2730	200	0-4-0	DE	Pilkington	12	58
2731	200	0-4-0	DE	Whitehead Iron & Steel	9	59
2732	200	0-4-0	DE	REA Ltd at Fire Service College, Moreton in Marsh	9	59
2733	400	-	Bo-Bo	African Manganese Guiana	12	58
2734	400	-	Bo-Bo	African Manganese Guiana	1	59
2735	400	-	Bo-Bo	African Manganese Guiana	1	59

2736	400	0-6-0	Janus	Appleby Frodingham at Tata Aldwarke	4	59
2737	400	0-6-0	Janus	Appleby Frodingham	4	59
2738	400	0-6-0	Janus	Appleby Frodingham	5	59
2739	400	0-6-0	Janus	PLA	5	59
2740	400	0-6-0	Janus	PLA at Tata Stocksbridge	6	59
2741	400	0-6-0	Janus	ICI	3	59
2742	400	0-6-0	Janus	ICI	3	59
2743	400	0-6-0	Janus	ICI	3	59
2744	220	0-6-0	DE	United Steels Ore Mining	5	60
2745	220	0-6-0	DE	NCB at South Devon Railway	8	60
2746	200	0-4-0	DE	Workington Iron and Steel	2	60
2747	200	0-4-0	DE	Workington Iron & Steel	2	60
2748	400	0-6-0	Janus	NCB at Churnet Valley Railway	9	59
2749	400	0-6-0	Janus	NCB	9	59
2750	400	0-6-0	Janus	Samuel Fox at Tata Aldwarke	6	59
2751	400	0-6-0	Janus	Samuel Fox	6	59
2752	400	0-6-0	Janus	Samuel Fox	6	59
2753	400	0-6-0	Janus	United Coke & Chemicals	6	59
2754	400	0-6-0	Janus	United Coke & Chemicals	2	60
2755	300	0-6-0	DE	PLA	9	59
2756	300	0-6-0	DE	PLA at Telford Steam Railway	10	59
2757	300	0-6-0	DE	PLA	10	59
2758	300	0-6-0	DE	PLA	11	59
2759	300	0-6-0	DE	PLA	10	59
2760	300	0-6-0	DE	PLA at Gloucester Warwickshire Railway	11	59
2761	300	0-6-0	DE	PLA	12	59
2762	300	0-6-0	DE	PLA	12	59
2763	300	0-6-0	DE	PLA	12	59
2764	400	0-6-0	Janus	Appleby Frodingham	12	59
2765	400	0-6-0	Janus	Appleby Frodingham	1	60
2766	440	0-6-0	Janus	Appleby Frodingham	1	60
2767	440	0-6-0	Janus	Appleby Frodingham	1	60
2768	440	0-6-0	Janus	Appleby Frodingham at Tata Scunthorpe	2	60
2769	300	0-6-0	DE	PLA	1	60
2770	300	0-6-0	DE	PLA	1	60
2771	230	0-6-0	DE	African Manganese Guiana at Matthews Ridge, Guyana	10	59
2772	440	0-6-0	Janus	Shelton Iron & Steel	8	60
2773	400	0-6-0	Janus	United Steels Ore D2	12	59
2774	275	0-4-0	DE2	Round Oak		60
2775	200	0-4-0	DE	Workington Iron & Steel	3	60

2776	200	0-4-0	DE	Workington Iron & Steel	3	60
2777	200	0-4-0	DE	Workington Iron & Steel	4	60
2778	200	0-4-0	DE	Workington Iron & Steel	3	60
2779	220	0-4-0	DE	Steetley Doloma	3	60
2780	220	0-4-0	DE	Shelton Iron & Steel	5	60
2781	200	0-4-0	DE	Pilkington	3	60
2782	200	0-4-0	DE	Pilkington at Llangollen Railway	3	60
2783	220	0-4-0	DE	Shelton Iron & Steel	5	60
2784	275	0-4-0	DE2	Round Oak	5	60
2785	275	0-4-0	DE2	Steel Peech & Tozer	6	60
2786	275	0-4-0	DE2	Steel Peech & Tozer	6	60
2787	440	0-6-0	Janus	Shelton Iron & Steel	3	61
2788	440	0-6-0	Janus	Appleby Frodingham at Tata Scunthorpe	10	60
2789	440	0-6-0	Janus	Appleby Frodingham	11	60
2790	440	0-6-0	Janus	Appleby Frodingham	11	60
2791	440	0-6-0	Janus	United Steels Ore Mining at 'Rocks by Rail' Rutland	4	62
2792	440	0-6-0	Janus	United Steels Ore Mining	2	61
2793	440	0-6-0	Janus	United Steels Ore Mining at Tata Scunthorpe	2	61
2794	440	0-6-0	Janus	Appleby Frodingham	9	61
2795	275	0-4-0	DE2	Round Oak	2	61
2796	275	0-4-0	DE2	Stewarts & Lloyds	7	60
2797	275	0-4-0	DE2	Stewarts & Lloyds	8	60
2798	440	0-6-0	Janus	Appleby Frodingham at Tata Stocksbridge	9	60
2799	440	0-6-0	Janus	Appleby Frodingham	10	60
2800	440	0-6-0	Janus	Brymbo Steel Works	3	62
2801	275	0-4-0	DE2	Stewarts & Lloyds	1	61
2802	220	0-4-0	DE	Barrow Steelworks	7	60
2803	220	0-4-0	DE	Barrow Steelworks	7	60
2804	220	0-4-0	DH	ICI	7	60
2805	220	0-4-0	DH	ICI	7	60
2806	220	0-4-0	DH	ICI	7	60
2807	220	0-4-0	DH	ICI	7	60
2808	220	0-4-0	DH	ICI	8	60
2809	170	0-4-0	DH	British Railways	10	60
2810	170	0-4-0	DH	British Railways	10	60
2811	170	0-4-0	DH	British Railways	10	60
2812	170	0-4-0	DH	British Railways at AFRPS Scunthorpe	10	60
2813	170	0-4-0	DH	British Railways at Peak Rail	11	60
2814	170	0-4-0	DH	British Railways	11	60
2815	170	0-4-0	DH	British Railways	12	60

2816	170	0-4-0	DH	British Railways	12	60
2817	170	0-4-0	DH	British Railways at Midland Railway Butterley	12	60
2818	170	0-4-0	DH	British Railways	1	61
2819	220	0-4-0	DE	Darwen & Mostyn	8	60
2820	170	0-4-0	DH	Pilkington	2	61
2821	275	0-4-0	DE2	Round Oak	3	61
2822	300	0-4-0	DH	RTB Ebbw Vale	2	61
2823	300	0-4-0	DH	RTB Ebbw Vale	2	61
2824	300	0-4-0	DH	RTB Ebbw Vale	3	63
2825	300	0-6-0	DH	RTB Llanwern at Tata, Skinningrove Works, Saltburn	4	61
2826	300	0-6-0	DH	RTB Llanwern	4	61
2827	300	0-6-0	DH	RTB Llanwern	5	61
2828	300	0-6-0	DH	RTB Llanwern	6	61
2829	300	0-6-0	DH	RTB Llanwern	7	62
2830	300	0-6-0	DH	RTB Llanwern	7	62
2831	300	0-6-0	DH	RTB Llanwern	1	62
2832	300	0-6-0	DH	RTB Llanwern at Tata Skinningrove Works, Saltburn	1	62
2833	300	0-6-0	DH	RTB Llanwern	2	62
2834	300	0-6-0	DH	RTB Llanwern	2	62
2835	300	0-6-0	DH	CEGB Skelton Grange	4	61
2836	300	0-6-0	DH	CEGB Skelton Grange	5	61
2837	300	0-6-0	DH	CEGB Skelton Grange	8	61
2838	170	0-4-0	DH	Pilkington	7	61
2839	300	0-6-0	DH	NCB	3	62
2840	300	0-4-0	DH	RTB Ebbw Vale	3	61
2841	300	0-4-0	DH	RTB Ebbw Vale	7	61
2842	300	0-4-0	DH	RTB Ebbw Vale	2	63
2843	170	0-4-0	DH	British Railways at National Rail Museum	9	61
2844	170	0-4-0	DH	British Railways	9	61
2845	170	0-4-0	DH	British Railways	10	61
2846	170	0-4-0	DH	British Railways	10	61
2847	170	0-4-0	DH	British Railways	10	61
2848	170	0-4-0	DH	British Railways	11	61
2849	170	0-4-0	DH	British Railways at Peak Rail	11	61
2850	170	0-4-0	DH	British Railways at Battlefield Line	11	61
2851	170	0-4-0	DH	British Railways at Peak Rail	11	61
2852	170	0-4-0	DH	British Railways	11	61
2853	220	0-4-0	DE	PLA	5	61
2854	220	0-4-0	DE	PLA at Llangollen Railway	5	61

2855	220	0-4-0	DE	PLA	5	61
2856	220	0-4-0	DE	PLA at private location	6	61
2857	220	0-4-0	DE	PLA	6	61
2858	220	0-4-0	DE	PLA	6	61
2859	275	0-4-0	DE2	Workington Iron & Steel	12	61
2860	275	0-4-0	DE2	Steel Peech & Tozer	2	62
2861	275	0-4-0	DE2	Steel Peech & Tozer	6	62
2862	170	0-4-0	DH	Hutchinson Estate & Dock	4	62
2863	440	0-6-0	Janus	Appleby Frodingham	4	62
2864	440	0-6-0	Janus	Appleby Frodingham	6	62
2865	440	0-6-0	Janus	Appleby Frodingham	7	62
2866	440	0-6-0	Janus	United Coke & Chemicals	7	62
2867	440	0-6-0	Janus	Brymbo	3	62
2868	440	0-6-0	Janus	Shelton Iron at Foxfield Railway	5	62
2869	220	0-4-0	DE	Shelton Iron	6	62
2870	220	0-4-0	DE	AEI £13,812	10	62
2871	220	0-6-0	DE	United Steels Ore	2	62
2872	220	0-6-0	DE	United Steels Ore Mining at 'Rocks by Rail' Rutland	2	62
2873	220	0-4-0	DE	Shelton Iron & Steel	4	64
2874	300	0-6-0	DH	NCB	2	63
2875	600	0-8-0	Taurus	Lent to BR as demonstrator and then dismantled	-	-
2876	440	0-6-0	Janus	AF	4	63
2877	440	0-6-0	Janus	Appleby Frodingham at AFRPS Scunthorpe	5	63
2878	440	0-6-0	Janus	Appleby Frodingham at Tata Llanelli	6	63
2879	275	0-4-0	DE2	Stewarts & Lloyds	11	62
2880	275	0-4-0	DE2	Stewarts & Lloyds	12	62
2881	275	0-4-0	DE2	Round Oak	5	62
2882	275	0-4-0	DE2	Round Oak	9	62
2883	275	0-4-0	DE2	Round Oak	3	63
2884	440	0-6-0	Janus	United Steels Ore Mining	11	62
2885	300	0-4-0	DE	Hired to RTB	-	-
2886	300	0-4-0	DE	Stanton Iron & Steel	6	61
2887	300	0-6-0	DH	NCB	2	63
2888	220	0-4-0	DE	Workington Iron & Steel	11	64
2889	300	0-6-0	DE	Park Gate Iron & Steel at Tata Aldwarke	11	62
2890	300	0-6-0	DE	Park Gate Iron & Steel at Tata Aldwarke	12	62
2891	300	0-6-0	DE	Park Gate Iron & Steel	3	63
2892	600	0-8-0	Taurus	RENFE Spain in Madrid Railway Museum	4	63
2893	600	0-8-0	Indus	RTB Llanwern	8	62

2894	600	0-8-0	Indus	Stewarts & Lloyds	8	62
2895	220	0-6-0	DH	Built not sold at Elsecar Railway	-	-
2896	220	0-6-0	DH	Built not sold; used by McCalls	-	-
2897	440	0-6-0	Janus	United Steels Ore	11	62
2898	440	0-6-0	Janus	Indian Fertilizer Corporation	11	63
2899	500	0-6-0	Janus	Appleby Frodingham	10	63
2900	500	0-6-0	Janus	Appleby Frodingham	11	63
2901	440	0-6-0	Janus	Appleby Frodingham	10	63
2902	440	0-6-0	Janus	Appleby Frodingham at Tata Scunthorpe	12	63
2903	500	0-6-0	Janus	Appleby Frodingham	1	64
2904	440	0-6-0	Janus	Steel Peech & Tozer at Tata Aldwarke	9	64
2905	300	0-6-0	DE	Park Gate Iron & Steel at Tata Aldwarke	3	63
2906	300	0-6-0	DE	Park Gate Iron & Steel at Tata Aldwarke	5	63
2907	300	0-6-0	DE	Park Gate Iron & Steel	6	63
2908	440	0-6-0	Janus	United Steels Ore Mining	7	63
2909	440	0-6-0	Janus	Appleby Frodingham	8	63
2910	375	0-6-0	DH	NCB	8	63
2911	375	0-6-0	DH	NCB	2	64
2912	375	0-6-0	DH	NCB	3	64
2913	375	0-6-0	DH	NCB	2	65
2914	440	0-6-0	Janus	Indian Fertilizer Corporation	11	63
2915	600	-	Olympus	Hindustan Steel	12	63
2916	600	-	Olympus	Hindustan Steel	12	63
2917	600	-	Olympus	Hindustan Steel	1	64
2918	600	-	Olympus	Hindustan Steel	1	64
2919	600	-	Olympus	Hindustan Steel	1	64
2920	600	-	Olympus	Hindustan Steel	2	64
2921	600	-	Olympus	Hindustan Steel	3	64
2922	600	-	Olympus	Hindustan Steel	5	64
2923	600	-	Olympus	Hindustan Steel	5	64
2924	600	-	Olympus	Hindustan Steel	6	64
2925	300	0-4-0	DE	Hindustan Steel	7	64
2926	300	0-4-0	DE	Hindustan Steel	7	64
2927	300	0-4-0	DE	Hindustan Steel	7	64
2928	300	0-4-0	DE	Hindustan Steel	7	64
2929	300	0-4-0	DE	Hindustan Steel	8	64
2930	350	0-6-0	DH	Southern Railway Peru	4	64
2931	350	0-6-0	DH	Southern Railway Peru	6	64
2932	350	0-6-0	DH	Southern Railway Peru	6	64
2935	440	0-6-0	Janus	Steel Peech & Tozer at Tata Aldwarke	9	64
2936	500	0-6-0	Janus	Appleby Frodingham	10	64

2937	500	0-6-0	Janus	Appleby Frodingham	11	64
2938	500	0-6-0	Janus	Appleby Frodingham at Tata Scunthorpe		65
2939	375	0-6-0	DH	NCB	3	65
2940	375	0-6-0	DH	NCB at Peak Rail	-	65
2942	220	0-6-0	DE	Brymbo	2	65
2943	500	0-6-0	Janus	Appleby Frodingham at Tata Scunthorpe	8	65
2944	440	0-6-0	Janus	Appleby Frodingham at Tata Aldwarke	8	65
2945	440	0-6-0	Janus	Appleby Frodingham at Tata Scunthorpe	8	65
2946	440	0-6-0	Janus	SPT	8	65
2947	440	0-6-0	Janus	Steel Peech & Tozer at Tata Aldwarke	8	65
2948	300	0-4-0	DH	Workington Iron & Steel	7	65
2949	300	0-4-0	DH	Workington Iron & Steel	7	65
2950	300	0-4-0	DH	Workington Iron & Steel	7	65
2951	300	0-4-0	DH	Workington Iron & Steel	9	65
2952	300	0-4-0	DH	Workington Iron & Steel at Stainmore Railway Kirby Stephen East	9	65
2953	275	0-4-0	DE2	Stewarts & Lloyds	-	65

Notes

1. Port of London Authority.
2. British Thomson Houston, part of the AEI Group.

Bibliography

The primary source of information for the history of the Yorkshire Engine Co. has been the records lodged in the Sheffield Archives. Most records cover the period from 1865 to the acquisition by United Steel in 1945. Only the progressive number book continues to 1965 and the order books to 1956. Items consulted include:

YEC 1-2 Progressive number book and order books (1–48), plus typed list of diesel locomotives.
YEC 3–5 Photograph albums and box of loose photographs of both locomotives and works interiors.
YEC 6–7 Technical plans and drawings.
YEC 8–15 Labour records for limited periods only.
YEC 16–20 Technical Records – principally engine weight books.
The board minutes (eight volumes) and various corporate and accounting records and balance sheets have also been read and are lodged separately under reference 1994/8.
United Steel Co. records (1994/15) are also held in the Sheffield Archives. The Managing Directors' Advisory Committee Minutes provided some information on Yorkshire Engine between 1945 and 1965.
Several Yorkshire Engine Catalogues were reviewed. They are undated and the dates given below are estimates: Industrial and Other Locomotives, c.1915; General Catalogue, c.1930; Standard Industrial Locomotives – Steam and Diesel, c.1951; 275hp DE, c.1961; 200hp DE ('Half Janus'), c.1956; 220hp DE, c.1960; 400hp DE 'Janus', c.1956; 300hp DH, c.1961; 600hp DH Taurus, c.1961; 200–275 DH, c.1963; Driver's Handbook – 300hp DE Shunting Locomotive.

Magazines (specific references are given in the endnotes)

Back Track, January 2006
Diesel Rail Traction
Emerson Bainbridge biography
Engineering
Fairlie Locomotive Part I, PC Dewhurst April 1962
Fairlie Locomotive Part II, PC Dewhurst and Harold Holcroft November 1966
House of Commons Select Committee, July 1873
Industrial Railway Record
Locomotive
Locomotive International
Locomotive Magazine
Locomotives
Locomotives on Roads
Modern Transport
Newcomen Society Paper
Pages Weekly, June 1906
Political & Economic Planning Report, 1951
Railway Gazette
Railway Magazine
Railway Modeller
Railway World

Samuel Fox Journal, 1951
Stephenson Locomotive Society Magazine
Times
Unisteel, October 1964
United Steel Newsletter – J. Compton article on Yorkshire Engine
Yorkshire Engine – The Sturrock & Sacré Years by Tony Vernon

Books

Archibald Sturrock, Pioneer Locomotive Engineer. T. Vernon. (The History Press 2007)
Articulated Locomotives. L. Wiener. (1930)
Beyer Peacock History. R. Hills & D. Patrick. (1972)
British Industrial Locomotives NCB 1967–9. (Industrial Railway Society 1970)
Cavalcade of Japanese Locomotives. (Locomotive History Society of Japan 1986)
Continent, Coalfield and Conservation – British Army Austerity. A.P. Lambert & J.C. Woods. (Industrial Railway Society 1991)
Diesel Shunter. C. Marsden. (Ian Allan 2003)
Fairlie Articulated Locomotives Vol.I. D. Binns. (Trackside Publications 2001)
Fairlie Locomotive. R. Abbott. (David & Charles 1970)
GNR Locomotive History Vol.I. N. Groves. (Railway Correspondence & Travel Society 1986)
Golden Age of Steam Locomotive Building. P. Atkins. (Atlantic 1999)
Great Central Railway Locomotives Vol.I. E.M. Johnson. (Irwell Press 1989)
Harry Pollitt. G. Hughes & D. Jackson. (1995)
Industrial Diesels. A.J. Booth. (Bradford Barton 1977)
Industrial Steam Locomotives – Lancashire & Cheshire. (Warwickshire Railway Society 1969)
Industrial Steam Locomotives (Illawarra District New South Wales). (Australian Railway History Society 1983)
Little Railways of South West Scotland. D.L. Smith. (David & Charles 1969)
Mechanical Power on Tramways. D.K. Clark. (1894)
Nasmyth Wilson & Co. J. Cantrell. (The History Press 2006)
Nitrate Railways Company Limited. D. Binns. (Trackside Publications 2007)
North British Railway. C. Hamilton Ellis. (Ian Allan 1959)
Railways of the Andes. B. Fawcett. (Plateway 1997)
Second Diesel Spotter's Guide. J.A. Pinkepank. (Kalmbach 1973)
Steam in Turkey. E. Talbot. (Continental Railway Circle 1982)
Steam Locomotives in Industry. (Industrial Locomotive Society 1967)
Steam Locomotion on Common Roads. W. Fletcher. (1891)
Steam on the RENFE. L.G. Marshall. (Macmillan 1965)
Stories & Sketches Relating to Yorkshire. J. Tomlinson. (1868)
The Scunthorpe Scene 1956–1986. J.J. Foreman. (Appleby Frodingham Railway Preservation Society)
Transcaucasian Railway and the Royal Engineers. R.A.S. Hennessey. (Trackside Publications 2004)
United Steel History 1918–1968. R. Peddie. (1969)
Vertical Boiler Locomotives. R. Abbott. (Oakwood 1989)

Index

'Austerity' locomotives 87-89, 102
Admiralty 27, 60, 79
AEI (Associated Electrical Industries) 96, 109, 118, 127, 130
African Manganese, Guyana 126-7, 129
Agricultural & Gen. Engineering 35
Akroyd Harold 56, 60, 72, 77, 82
Aldwarke 6, 108, 116
Allan straight link motion 23
Aluminium Union, Jamaica 108, 126
Anderson, Col. 22
Anglo Chilean & Nitrate Co. 37-8
Ankleshwar Pardi Railway 37, 39
Appleby Frodingham 79, 80, 83-85, 87, 90, 103-6, 108, 115, 118, 122, 130, 132
Appleby Frodingham Railway Preservation Society 134
Appleby Iron Works 32, 69
Argentina 20
Armstrong Whitworth 64
Auckland Lord, see Eden Hon W.G.
Australia 20, 23, 39, 41, 47-49, 65, 96, 129
Avonside 13, 20, 22, 64, 79

Babcock y Wilcox 65, 68
Bagnall, W.G. 70, 79
Bainbridge, Emerson 46, 49, 50, 52, 60
Banks, Col. 82, 87
Barcelona 29
Barker, T.R. 8, 11, 20
Barrow Hill Roundhouse 87, 90
Barrow Steelworks 115
Barry Railway 64
Belfast Holywood & Bangor Railway 21, 136
Belgian Street Tramway 28
Belgium 22-4, 28-9, 72, 134
Bengal Nagpur Railway 65, 68
Beyer Peacock 14, 30, 35, 44, 58, 70, 78, 82

Binns, Donald 26, 35
Bolton Iron & Steel, 44
Bombay Baroda & Central India Railway, 37, 39
Brazil 23
Briddon, Peter 119
British Railways – Western Region 87, 91, 93, 118
British Thomson Houston (BTH) 96-98, 103, 109, 118, 121, 126-7
British Transport Commission 103, 118
Brymbo Steelworks 105, 108, 115
Buenos Ayres Great Southern Railway 18-20, 32, 37, 102
Buenos Ayres Western Railway 58
Bury Port & Gwendraeth Railway 23, 35

Calder Hall 96
Cammell Charles & Co. 16, 21, 30, 43, 46-7, 49
Canto-Gallo Railway 23
Central Electricity Generating Board (CEGB) 111
Central Railway of Paraguay (Ferrocarril Presidente Carlos Antonio Lopez) 93-4
Central Railway of Peru 65, 66, 73
Central Uruguay Railway 23
Chadwick, David 8
Charles Tayleur & Co. 8
Chattendon & Upnor Railway 42-3
Chatterley Whitfield 34, 46
Chemin de Fer Andalouse 68
Chesterfield Special Cylinders 8
Chilean Northern Railway (Antofagasta Chile & Bolivia Railway) 93, 94, 97, 99
Christmas, John (Jack) 94, 98, 102, 104, 111, 113, 120, 125, 126, 134
Clark, T.F. 45, 49
Clark, D.K. 28
Clayton Equipment 80-1, 118

Clayton Shuttleworth 49
Clugston 115
Coal Cutters 46
Cockerill, John 22
Compton, Joseph 82, 91, 98, 102-3, 125, 130, 132-4
Corus 104, 113, 116-7, 133-4
Craven Brothers 11
Crawley & Meynier 16, 17, 23
Crown Agents 52, 65, 103
Cummins 106, 108-9, 127, 130-1

Darfield Main Colliery 21
Davey Paxman 97, 118
Distington Engineering 100, 105-6, 117
Dublin & South Eastern Railway 58
Dubs 14, 30, 44

Earl Fitzwilliam 21, 79
East & West Junction Railway 26
East Indian Railway 11, 13, 16, 30-1
Eastern Bengal Railway 76
Eccles Slag 112, 117
Eden, Hon. W.G. 8, 10-11, 20
Edinburgh, Duke of 3
Elsecar Steam Railway 122, 133
Embsay & Bolton Abbey Railway 87
Esso 118

Fairbairns 14
Fairlie Locomotives 22-27, 30, 32, 35, 37-9, 41-2, 50, 56, 66
Fairlie, Robert 22-3
Felixstowe Railway 32
Fenton, W. 24-5
Ferrymead Museum, New Zealand 30
First World War 46, 54, 58, 60, 62-5, 79, 82
Foggo, Watson 49, 50, 52, 55
Fox, Douglas 23

158

Gilling, A.H. 60, 64, 70, 72, 76
Goldendale Iron 58, 96
Gooch, Sir Daniel 8
Gorton Works 44
Grand Compagnie de Luxembourg 24-5
Grand Trunk of Canada 14
Great Central Railway (See also Manchester Sheffield & Lincolnshire Railway) 12, 43-4, 48-9, 54
Great Eastern Railway 25, 30, 137
Great Indian Peninsula Railway 11, 13, 37, 50, 52, 82
Great Northern Railway (GNR) 6, 8, 11, 13-15, 20-1, 73, 75
Great Western Railway (GWR) 8, 43, 64-5, 70, 72, 91
Greenly, Henry 73, 76
Gresley, Sir Nigel 69
GWR Pannier Tanks 91

Hallsberg-Motola- Mjobly Railway 24
Hampson, Robert 10, 13, 14, 17, 20, 22, 29, 34, 36-7, 43, 45-52
Harley, C.B. 49, 63, 65, 69, 78
Harrison, Company Secretary 34-36
Hatcham Iron Works 22
Haulage Engines 46, 54-6, 60, 62, 64, 76, 80
Hawthorn Leslie 64, 79-80, 82, 89
Hepworth Iron 46-7, 96
HH the Gaekwar's State Railway 37, 39
Hindustan Steel, Durgapur 126-9, 132
Hoylake & Birkenhead Tramway & Railway Co. 32-33
Huddersfield 29
Hull & Barnsley Railway 51-6, 65
Hulse, W.W. 14, 20
Hunslet Engine Co. 87, 91, 93, 96, 102, 134
Hunt & Sacré 11, 20, 22
Hunter, Arthur 133

ICI (Imperial Chemical Industries) 107, 118
Imperial Ottoman Railway 32-3
Indian Fertilizer Corporation 108, 126
Indian State Railways 30, 37, 57, 59
Iquique 25, 56

James Cross of St Helens 22
Japanese Government Railway 19-21

Jenkinson, H.C. 48
Jenkinson, Sydney 64, 77
Jodhpur Railway 80
John Brown 30, 79
John Fowler of Leeds 11, 14
John Summers 99-101, 117, 146
Jones, Captain Charles Frederick Ward 55-56, 60, 62, 64
Jones, Sir Fredrick 52-3, 55, 60, 63
Jones, Sir Walter Benton 63, 82-3
Junin Railway 39, 41, 139

Kelham Island Industrial Museum 7, 97
Kerr Stuart 64, 70
Kitson, George P. 16
Kitsons 10, 14, 16, 45, 55, 58, 64
Kiveton Park Colliery 21, 36

Lancashire & Yorkshire Railway 30, 32, 137
Lancashire Derbyshire & East Coast Railway 58
Lancashire Steel 85, 87, 100, 117
Ledger, Bernard 6, 94, 111, 134
Lidgett Colliery 46, 49
Livesey Son & Henderson 66, 96
Locomotive Manufacturers' Association (LMA) 32, 76-7, 82
London Brighton & South Coast Railway 43, 50, 58
London Chatham & Dover Railway 11
London North Eastern Railway (LNER) 44-5, 55, 63, 65, 69, 72, 96, 98
Londonderry & Coleraine 22
Longmoor Military Railway 42

Malta 42
Manchester Sheffield & Lincolnshire Railway (MSLR) 8, 10-11, 27, 43-4, 49
Manning Wardle 10, 79
Maryport & Carlisle Railway 65, 68
McCalls 130, 133
McNulty, Pat 65, 88, 91, 93
Metropolitan Railway 45, 47, 54, 56, 58, 69, 72
Mexican Railway 23-24
Mexican Southern Railway 37-8
Meyer-type articulated locomotives 42, 51, 56, 66, 73
Midland Railway 44
Moira Colliery 43, 46
Montero Bros, Lima 25-6
Moore, W.H. 77

Moscow Kursk Railway 15
Moscow Ryazan 14-17
Moss, C.H. 52-3, 55-6, 63-4
Motor House 50, 52-4
Mount Morgan Railway 47

Nasmyth Wilson 30, 64, 77, 78
National Coal Board (NCB) 85, 90, 103, 118
National Railway Museum 121-2
Neath & Brecon Railway 44
Neilsons 10, 14, 35
New Zealand Railways 30-31
Nitrate Railways 66, 69, 78, 91
North British Railway 55-7, 63, 69-70, 93-4, 96
North West Gas 109, 118
Northern Railway Spain 65
Nunnery Colliery 46, 79

Oume Railway Park, Tokyo 19-20

Packe Col. 11
Parker, Thomas 44
Peak Rail 92, 97, 132
Peddie, R. 102, 129, 132
Perkins Loftus 22, 26-8, 30, 34
Peruvian Railways 25, 32, 93, 127
Phillips, J.D.R. 53, 55, 60
Pilkington 118, 123
Pillau 16
Pirie, James 29
Pisagua 25-6
Pollitt, Harry 44, 48
Port of London Authority (PLA) 105, 107-8, 118, 120
Poti-Tiflis Railway 17-18, 23, 26, 136-7
Poultney, Edward Cecil 72-75, 78
Puerto Cabello & Valencia Railway 57, 59, 65

Queensland Government Railway 23, 39-40

Rack Rails 47, 49, 79
Railway Foundry 10
Ravenglass & Eskdale Railway 73, 75-6
RENFE 32, 35, 65, 78, 125-6
Robert Stephenson 14, 30, 64, 79, 83-4, 89
Robinson, J.G. 44
Rohlikund & Kumaon Railway 80
Rolls Royce 109, 111, 115, 121, 124-5, 127, 132-4

159

Romney Hythe & Dymchurch Railway (RH&DR) 73-6
Rothervale Collieries 46, 52, 58, 60, 67, 69, 79-80, 85
Rotherham 6, 11, 17, 82, 97, 108, 116, 132-3
RTB (Richard Thomas & Baldwins) 111, 113-4, 117
Ryazan Uralsk Railway 14

Sacré, Alfred 8, 10, 11, 13, 14, 16, 20, 22
Sacré, Charles 8, 10, 13, 17, 20, 27, 44
Sacré, Edward 11, 20, 22, 26-30, 32, 37
Samuel Fox 82, 85, 87, 90, 99-102, 108, 117, 132
Scunthorpe 7, 103, 105, 108, 112, 117, 133
Second World War 69, 70, 76, 81, 93
Seeley & Wood oil engine 60
Sentinel 108, 130, 132-3
Seville & Malaga Railway 11
Sharp, Stewart 14, 22, 32, 35, 43, 45, 58
Sheffield –Victoria Hotel 10
Sheffield & Rotherham Bank 17
Sheffield Telegraph 130
Sheffield Chief Constable 14
Sheffield Tramways 29
Shelton Iron & Steel 108, 117
Sindi Punjab & Delhi Railway 37
Snowdon Mountain Railway 47, 49
South Eastern & Chatham Railway 50, 58
South Yorkshire Chemicals 118-9
South Yorkshire Railway 8
Southern & Western Railway of Queensland 23
Southern Railway of Peru 127-128
St Austell & Pentewan Railway 42
Stanton Iron 108, 111
Staveley Iron & Chemicals 111, 112, 117

Steam Tender Locomotives 8, 13, 64, 73-75
Steel Peech & Tozer 44, 69, 71, 78-9, 82, 85, 91-2, 97-8, 100, 108, 116-7
Steetley 80-1, 117
Stewarts & Lloyds 100-1, 111, 115, 117
Stirling, Matthew 45, 51, 55, 63
Stirling, Patrick 11, 13, 15
Stocksbridge 82, 104, 108, 132
Sturrock, Archibald 6, 8, 10-11, 13-17, 20, 73-5
Sturrock, Gordon 17
Sugden, Edward 37, 48, 52
Swansea Tramways 28
Sweden 23-24

Taff Vale Railway 58, 64
Taltal 25, 58
Tambov Koslov Railway 14-15
Thomas Firth 43, 79
Thomas Hill 133
Transcaucasian Railway 18, 21, 26, 35

United Coke & Chemicals 85, 108, 117
United Steel Managing Director's Advisory Committee (MDAC) 102, 129, 132-4
United Steel Ore Mining Branch 84-5, 87, 108, 117

Vaucamps M 28
Vickers, Thomas (and related cos) 36, 43, 46, 52, 70, 79
Victorian Railways 20
Vulcan Foundry 8, 44-5, 96

Walker, George Blake 46, 52
Walschaerts valve gear 23, 42
War Office (Secretary of State for War) 42-3, 60
Watkin, ERS 102-3, 129-132
Western Springs Railway, New Zealand 30-1
Wharncliffe Collieries 34, 46
Wheatley, Thomas 29
Whitworth, James 14
Wigtownshire Railway 29, 35
Willans, K.W. 55, 60
Wilson, George 10
Wingerworth Iron 21
Wood, Alf 133
Woodhouse & Rixon 43
Workington Harbour & Docks 84, 86, 100
Workington Iron & Steel 84, 91, 100, 118

Yorkshire Engine – Car manufacturing 50-63
Yorkshire Engine – Marine Engines 27, 30
Yorkshire Engine – Type I 83-8, 90, 93, 102
Yorkshire Engine – Type IV 83-4
Yorkshire Engine – Type V 83-7, 100
Yorkshire Engine – Tramway Locomotives 28-32
Yorkshire Engine BR Class 02 118, 121-3
Yorkshire Engine BR Class 15 118, 121
Yorkshire Engine DE1 98
Yorkshire Engine DE2 98, 100, 101
Yorkshire Engine DE3 98
Yorkshire Engine DE4 98-102
Yorkshire Engine Hydraulics 109-111
Yorkshire Engine Indus 111, 114-117
Yorkshire Engine Janus 89, 103-109, 111, 115-121, 126-7, 132
Yorkshire Engine Olympus 127-8, 130
Yorkshire Engine Taurus 109, 111, 121-126
Yorkshire Engine Zeus 127, 130

If you are interested in purchasing other books published by The History Press, or in case you have difficulty finding any History Press books in your local bookshop, you can also place orders directly through our website

www.thehistorypress.co.uk